Dream Interpretation

Find Meaning in the Messages of Your Subconscious Mind

(Understanding Your Own Imaginings and Mysterious Dreams Language Interpreted)

James Bates

Published By **Simon Dough**

James Bates

Dream Interpretation: Find Meaning in the Messages of Your Subconscious Mind (Understanding Your Own Imaginings and Mysterious Dreams Language Interpreted)

ISBN   978-1-998038-34-3

Legal & Disclaimer

Table Of Contents

Chapter 1: Psychological Reality

Did you understand you have had been given an Inner Story? Just as you've got an Outer, Waking Reality Story, you moreover may also have, within the form of your dreams, an Inner Reality Story. However, in contrast to ebook or film topics, one's Inner Story is each malleable and never-finishing. As the Dream Alchemist, you may skillfully song your goals/Inner Story, making countless modifications to be combined and paired to be able to create your essential life.

And due to the truth goals screen what need to, by using the newbie dream analyst, mistakenly be interpreted as myriad hodgepodge elements of 1's All-That-Is, it turns into essential for a extra comprehensively-formatted organizational machine than easy word definitions. Therefore, this manuscript gives a extra technically-correct running definition: Dreams are Reality Framework Two's real or metaphorically-condensed model of Reality

Framework One's spacious gift highbrow charge weather.

Dreams can display expansive, extensive realities which might be internal our reap—realities that the Outer-Ego/Reasoning Mind might also furthermore categorically reject due to highbrow bias. Yet, our innate intellectual and intuitive talents need now not be competition. Instead, we've got the energy to combine every for an considerable lifestyles. Because of the profound attracting energy of the Present Positive and the lifestyles of unknown, Probable Realities, there may be usually the possibility for selection:

It's your approach to your karma—your present situation, that determines an final results. You've the power to transform your existence proper now. Just preserve the channels open and feature agree with. If you can live effective, any proscribing existence situation may be transformed. You always have the choice to maintain the channels open; to connect with some issue more than you presently agree with your self to be. ~ Kuan Yin

Know that your first-class dream rendition of what passed off within the so-known as beyond is as legitimate as you believe it to be! When you operate your Free Will to bear in mind a pleasing model of your past, you increasingly more actualize it as part of your present waking reality memories and experience. Such expansive visions in dreams showcase that your gift has aligned with one in all your maximum and most innovative variations of your self. Beyond that, you definitely want to teach your waking thoughts to first rate recall the pleased feeling of that expansive imaginative and prescient! When carrying out this, all areas of your lifestyles can shift, developing limitless manifestation opportunities!

Once, I dreamt I emerge as taking my little one and his friends for a swim in a neighbor's pool. Jumping in for a second time, I couldn't help but word that what changed into at first a hairline crack spanning the lowest of the pool modified into now abruptly widening. Everyone out of the pool!

Initially blaming me for the broken pool, the neighbor have end up furious. Countering his accusations, I spoke back, You ought to have diagnosed all along this pool have become destined to fail!

Nodding in settlement, the neighbor reluctantly concurred.

Contemplating the dream, I knew it come to be a metaphor for personal and societal paradigm recognition shifts—that interest of the Dynamic System of Consciousness taking area among Reality Framework One and Two could balance the over-advanced, remoted Outer-Ego of Framework One.

In the begin, Outer Ego (the outward-turning organizer of records-enter from Framework One) and its proclivity to differentiate among itself and the opposite, modified into in its infancy and Inner Ego (the inward-turning organizer of facts-enter from Framework Two) have emerge as the dreamer of its truth. Thus, no separation existed between thyself and thy tree. Nor, did it exist amongst thyself and thy serpent or thy stars and galaxies.

And inside the beginning there was wonderment—devotional appreciation for one's self and surroundings! Like a little one marveling at its big toe or a lover entranced with their love, it end up this intensity of emotion enabling the very existence strain.

Wonderment equals alignment with the Life Force!

Additionally, no separation existed among humanity and its archetypes. S/He grow to be the tree! S/He became the flower! S/He changed into the chalice! S/He changed into the typhoon! S/He have become the sound and the mild! And so it have emerge as that the archetypes were additionally related to wonderment and the allowing of the in-built recovery strain that would in the end be

5

forgotten by using the usage of the isolated ego:

I see the folds of her garment, all over again, so thick and complicated. Kuan Yin is right here looking a lotus. However, she's more than looking at it; she's being with it, meditating upon it, appreciating it. She's centered very carefully on the lotus as even though she is conversing with it. It's an thrilling element to appearance Kuan Yin referring to a flower so carefully. Now, the lotus is floating away.~ Oracle of Compassion: the Living Word of Kuan Yin

Whereas, the individuality of the Outer-Ego/Reasoning Mind extra intently denotes the male/father archetype, the oneness of the Inner-Ego/All-That-Is/detail greater carefully denotes the female/mom archetype. As historic traditions associate the lotus and one of a kind vessel-ordinary flora with the girl/mom archetype, mankind's diminishing functionality to connect to its Inner-Ego/All-That-Is/element, (thru over improvement of the Outer-Ego), is symbolized with the resource of Kuan Yin's metaphor of the lotus floating away.

Because of the individual of desires (and their proximity in the All-That-Is), however, this sacred connection grow to be never surely deserted. Memory of its magnanimity however lives internal no matter Outer-Ego's obvious slim perceptions of itself.

Similar to the early zygotes first cleavage signifying the begin of the fetus, the Outer-Ego (Reality Framework One) often separated itself from the All-The-Is (Reality Framework Two), no matter the reality that taking with it some distance flung reminiscences of its connection with the archetypes. Because of recognition's regular, innate proclivity to balance Reality Framework One and Two, but, on every occasion Outer-Ego becomes too isolated, archetypes internal Reality Framework Two will resurface in dreams.

My dream of swinging precariously thru the air; imprisoned internal some large hen cage

(Framework One), served as such an example. Pleading to be launched with what I sensed changed right right into a stress beyond something I should ever remember (Framework Two), I eventually located out my cries had lengthy beyond unheard. Only after by means of using some way growing my diploma of recognition, did this pressure ultimately pay hobby me; permitting me my freedom! Thus, even as Reality Framework One and Two are vibrationally-aligned, the character can start to heal.

Humanity is aware at the maximum intimate ranges that on the identical time as attainment of individuality and its myriad modern-day expressions via development of Outer-Ego attention have end up constantly the goal, the species would in the end gather a element in which the disastrous potentials of its over-development should outweigh any further exploration in that direction.

However, the evolution of the species has no beginning or quit—nice seasons of existence.

And in this, our wintry weather of existence, we stock the lamplight of recognition even as delving ever deeper into the mystery of our becoming. Because of the profound appeal power of the mind and its ability to get right of entry to its trade tiers of interest: i.E. Psychological Reality Framework Two, there without prevent are avenues for decision of one's waking fact.

As virtually every body is on a journey of self-love and hobby, one constantly has the possibility to enjoy (through trance and dreams), the Inner Self's large array of understanding that might allow for a more revel in of being, thereby recuperation any distrust generated via the use of the isolated Outer-Ego. Love is popularity and to surely love yourself is elegance of that that is your essence: the multidimensional selves of Reality Framework Two. Will Outer-Ego wake up to the electricity of its twin Inner-Ego concept and emotional methods, knowing that it this innate connection growing all reality?

Similar to the mind of a toddler, the deep inquisitiveness of a Wondrous State of Mind fosters a interest to recognize the secrets of the universe. Indeed, this Wondrous State can not be finished without a superb level of recall within the Grand Plan: that, without exception, definitely anyone is invested on this, our great expansion of focus. The mixture of marvel and take into account creates an openness for receiving all devices the universe has to offer.

Paramount to this marveling tool is the improvement of a particular form of popularity: perceiving a given item or occasion in a deep and personal manner. You at once "assume your self there", moving in trade and appreciating that that you are also looking. Momentarily liberated from the artificial area-time of waking reality, you quite consequences stumble upon your private divinity.

There are those unlucky beliefs, however, which can as a minimum briefly, undermine one's enthusiasm. If one becomes too diminished of their mindset; they may come to consider in a totally-romanticized justification for suffering: that struggling brings one in the direction of salvation. Or, that suffering by way of using a few method validates one's life. Combined with the "no longer enough", "better than" and "survival of the fittest" beliefs, this attitude can balloon right right into a hurricane of misunderstanding, doubtlessly inflicting one to make lifestyles-sabotaging picks. Look past the typhoon; figuring out only your most expansive potentials. Through marveling on the highlights; the inspiring moments of your lifestyles, you start the technique of wondering yourself to an area of peace and prosperity.

It is one's multi-dimensional mind modalities permitting one to psychically feel and experience past any obstacles. The venture for humanity, then, is to make use of this synthetic area-time scaffolding for effective focused motive. Just as proceeding proper for others absolutely magnetizes expansive electricity, feeling actual appreciation for the existing creates a powerfully extremely good enchantment pressure. Therefore, even in case you attempt for some component extra on your lifestyles, famend the miracle of your present reality.

From considerate and cautious reviewing, you can come to recognize your styles; thereby higher clarifying and aligning the connection among your waking and dream worlds. Such a method may be a sturdy catalyst for focusing your hobby (through affirmation and visualization) upon attracting those realities flawlessly-tailored on your particular karma and dreams. You may have already discovered the advantages of your efforts: small and then likely extra full-size powerful sports beginning to unfold because the layers of Self are transformed.

The order of the universe is measured in frequency. For example, each galaxy; each celestial formation has its super Power

Spectrum Signature. This frequency-order is also biologically-expressed within the (at least) 5 brainwave frequencies forming human focus. In fact, sound asleep and dreaming represent waking-self's transition from one's faster waking/beta-thoughts EEG Periodicity to the slower trance/alpha-mind, to the even slower, sleep, dreaming/theta-thoughts.

Quantum Physics Entanglement Theory states that two particles which have formerly been linked and are then separated have an ability to speak with and impact every one-of-a-kind. Even contemporary unimaginably prolonged distances apart, they may all the time have the ability to modify each distinct. Because the two Psychological Reality Frameworks are entangled, the great, depth and fee of gadgets and sports in Framework One will come into balance with the terrific, depth and fee of gadgets and activities in Framework Two, influencing manipulation abilities in Framework One.

The Dynamic System of Consciousness consists of number one styles of perceptual/organizational skills occurring between the two mediums of recognition: Psychological Reality Framework One: The Outer-Ego/beta/Reasoning Mind in famous linear perceptions/organizations and Psychological Reality Framework Two: the Inner-Ego/alpha-theta-delta/All-That-Is Mind in most instances nonlinear perceptions/companies. Within this EEG Human Behavioral Spectrum of Consciousness: i.E. Quantum Flux Spectrum of Consciousness is computerized, simultaneous. Mind-to-rely linear and nonlinear interactions/companies normal with the Universal Laws of Attraction, Consciousness Equilibrium and Quantum Fluctuations.

Regard this: your waking Reality Framework One as a sacred present—a temporary anchor interior an ever-transferring universe. Skillful manage can result in new private and/or mass understandings and reprioritizing: an expansive shift concerning every Framework

One and Two. You own Seven Innate Forces of Becoming. Before your the front into the arena, there was your resonance: unique vibrations springing from deeply held ideals. Resonance is simply one of the seven innate forces influencing one's unique manner of turning into. The following lists all seven: Beliefs, Free Will, Emotions, Vibration (Tonal Wave-Mass Resonance), Imagination, Intuition and the Creative Force Energy. One's Seven Innate Forces are synergistic: that they'll be greater than the sum of their additives. What one believes, as an example, will in element have an effect on one's feelings, vibration, creativeness, and so forth. How skillfully you manipulate them will decide your command of these fundamental forces.

You could in all likelihood don't forget your dreams are but random snippets intruding upon your non violent sleep. Another method is you surmise that thru absolutely defining dream symbols, you'll arrive at appropriate solutions for what they're looking to deliver.

However, the above strategies will in the long run fail to provide the deeper answers.

And as desires, extra regularly than now not, speak metaphorically, understand that humans have, all through their lifetimes, assigned their specific meanings to symbols appearing of their goals. Therefore, blanket dream image definitions might not always provide genuine sufficient interpretations for what one's desires are trying to impart. Relaters of the ecstatic dance of interest: i.E. Consciousnesses pirouetting inside its self-created Quantum Flux Spectrum, goals offer a glimpse into one's internal most knowledge.

Precursors to what may also additionally need to eventually be attracted into waking fact, desires play a important role inside the Deep Dream Psychology—discovery one's motivations for introduction in their fact. Whether one regards the dream nation as Framework Two, the Subconscious Mind, the Inner Self, the Higher Self, Sacred Vessel, the All-That-Is, the World of Dreams or the

Nonlinear Self, this manuscript from proper here on will commonly check with it as Psychological Reality Framework Two. It is this issue of Self harboring reputation of all thoughts, devices and activities having ever existed. Indeed, this vessel of all subjects is lively 24/7, offering the very manna of existence.

A select out employer of scientists now regard interest and its super complexities as a Dynamic System. For the features of this manuscript, interest is defined as a self-contained, Dynamic System, advancing (inside its self-created Quantum Flux Spectrum) from obvious chaos to tentative equilibrium. Because of the catalytic (and probably stress-inducing) effect of Framework One's included evaluation, a non-prevent equilibrium is probably no longer sustainable. Indeed, in the Great Expansion of Consciousness, the best constant is alternate itself.

It is that this indefiniteness stimulating Outer Ego's look for eternal solutions. When it turns into apparent that Framework One isn't capable of provide sufficient answers, Outer-Ego's seemingly unsolvable conundrum stimulates a name to motion from Framework Two's nonlinearly-prepared dream global.

Static models of consciousness at least allow for a sequential evolution of recovery. The Deep Dream Psychology Model implies, but, that from shipping to loss of life, there are non-stop quantum adjustments of recognition via the presentation of possibly chaos in Framework One stimulating dream answers in Framework Two. Eventually, Framework Two's dream solutions will create an alteration in Outer-Ego's waking truth, causing it to move into tentative equilibrium/reconciliation with Framework Two. Ameliorating the ability pressure stemming from Framework One's evaluation, is one's unfastened will to get right of get admission to to their Inner Integrity: the internal calm beneficial aid that each one the time dwells inside. Daily meditation, setting ahead the triumphing exceptional, communing with nature or taking note of calming music are a few techniques to get right of get entry to to this buffering u . S . Of thoughts.

Unlike the Outer-Ego, which interfaces and organizes one's waking-global's sequential records, the Inner-Ego interfaces with and organizes nonlinear statistics inside the trance and dream worlds. Thus while dreaming, one enters a parallel realm wherein all possibilities look ahead to to be actualized into cloth form, possibly even glimpsing the large variety of objects and sports dwelling inside the All-That-Is. When dreaming, you will be drawn into exceptional worlds reflective of your personal pursuits and values. Each day on the same time as moving lower back from your theta (goals) to beta (waking) consciousness, you've make the selection to be part of that that you've attracted from All-That-Is into this, your waking fact. Otherwise, you'd certainly awaken in a few different body in a few specific reality.

Thus, the Deep Dream Psychology analytical and journaling technique defines dreams as: Reality Framework Two's nonlinear, in wellknown allegorical expressions of integration and amplification of strength tiers of attention inside the Quantum Flux Spectrum of Consciousness. Such expressions can display real or metaphorically-condensed gadgets and activities from Reality Framework One's spacious present intellectual price weather or the All-That-Is.

The following are twelve personal benefits to be acquired from desires:

1. To offer expansive notion/identity exchange stories for those now not serving one's notable hobbies.

2. To warn of capability threat.

three. To reprogram the mobile memory.

4. To broaden one's Hybrid Intellect/Emotionalism critical for the manipulation of depend.

five. To be part of the isolated ego with the All-That-Is.

6. To provide consciousness of one's Inner Sound of Matter/Inner Light/without end-robust Inner Integrity.

7. To elucidate the infinite factors of one's All-That-Is, in conjunction with Probable Selves/Realities.

eight. To elucidate mind-to-depend techniques thru immediately actualizations in Framework One in region of now not on time actualizations in Framework Two.

nine. To offer popularity of the Everlasting Legitimacy of the Soul.

10.To screen Superposition/Wave Function of the Universe—that all degrees of reputation exist concurrently.

11.To display the Quantum Flux Spectrum of Consciousness.

12.To screen Consciousness Quantum Entanglement: the understanding degree of manipulation of keep in mind in Framework Two equals the skills stage of manipulation of count number in Framework One.

Chapter 2: The Human EEG Behavioral

While honestly each person is absolutely particular, they percentage the identical great problem of focus. The air getting into their lungs is the identical this is breathed inside and outside by using manner of others.

It cycles thru the bloodstream, supporting to help cellular and organ function. While all of us has comparable perceptual skills, their precise observations allow for an individualistic revel in of their surroundings.

That private perceptions manage reality is substantiated thru what is termed, (inside the have a look at of Physics) the observer effect in which the observer, through assessment and/or size, alters the phenomenon being observed.

As all of us's, precise remark creates its personal space-time (because of this, Consciousness Space-Time), the identical is right for vicinity-time itself. Because of the

Observer Effect, remark of said and unknown devices and activities in desires creates the profound possibility (via the dreamer's precise interpretations), to stabilize, indeed rise up, specific devices and sports into waking fact. In these and plenty of distinct techniques, all people and the whole thing is mounted.

The universe we inhabit is consequently not accidental. Everything is, in a few manner, associated, beneficial. Expanding upon Entanglement Theory, Superposition is the concept that while items and activities may additionally seem to exist in a single kingdom or any other, the medium of simultaneity binds All-That-Is.

In humans, thoughts pastime ordinary with that of mirror neurons has been located in the pre-motor cortex, the supplementary motor vicinity, the number one somatosensory cortex and the inferior parietal cortex. As is well-documented, a human mom will spontaneously lactate upon listening to the cries of her toddler.

Some men, then again, have been recognized to extend what have been known as sympathetic difficult work pains and certainly one of a kind symptoms that, at the least in element, mirror their accomplice's being pregnant experience. This manifestation is normally referred to as "Couvade Syndrome" or "Sympathetic Pregnancy".

That we are difficult-stressed out to empathize with the pleasure and ache of others indicates that we're basically a cooperative, compassionate species. Moreover, reflect neurons end up even extra crucial at the same time as information the mind's tendency to fill-within the most probable conditions. And on the equal time as they're very important, they incorporate definitely one factor of reputedly endless organic records that the mind have to machine every day.

Other components are precise differing interstitial coronary coronary coronary heart rhythms that have been determined to correspond to essential feelings of affection or anger.

These underlying rhythms can be interpreted via the mind as both fitness or contamination going on inside the body. The mind will then reply to this data; robotically releasing what it deems as an appropriate frame chemicals. Endorphins and L-dopamine, brought about with the resource of particular emotions and activities, are constantly released via complicated neurotransmitters.

Cascading in some unspecified time in the future of the body, they'll transform ones very cell frame form. While commonly considered a way wherein neurons communicate with every first-rate through electro-chemical pathways, studies on reminiscence has unearthed in all likelihood as many mysteries as solutions. Because of the human mind's inexorable connection with the evolution of the soul, this courting also can all the time remain elusive to the sector of generation.

One problem is positive. What is generally called the thoughts isn't always limited within the organic organism known as the mind. Rather, it acts because the capacitor within the Quantum Flux Spectrum of Consciousness; a wave train like no distinct. When it includes attention, but, there's energy inner electricity; waves interior waves:

"Hope, I heard simultaneously even as you requested the question about the brainwave frequency tiers, Kuan Yin responding over your question. At the instant of your query, Kuan Yin had said, 'You imply defenses, the layers you're taking to maintain to the soul'", relayed Lena.

"You have," continued Kuan Yin, "as a minimum five brainwave frequency stages for our survival. They are the included defenses of human recognition. They, (much like the layers, auras in the course of the body) constitute layers of focus."

"Kuan Yin is displaying me the layers of density on our planet," persevered Lena. "They can be compared to the layers (of electricity, karma) coating our our bodies. The numerous brainwaves help us to go beyond, beneath the layers of karma. She is displaying me radio waves and microwaves. There are all types of waves, all of the time. The human thoughts can get proper of entry to certain waves at superb times…You understand I can't intervene with karma. The karmic cycle is in reality. However, you can ride karma like a wave. I genuinely have the equipment and all people can select out to make use of them to enhance their lives. Sometimes the waves are small. Sometimes the waves are massive.

In order to help others, one want to learn how to assist oneself."~ Oracle of Compassion: the Living Word of Kuan Yin

Regard each concept as a unit of energy stored inside the mind. That there are multiple likely selves to draw upon for information, this storage of statistics is constructing order; therefore appearing as a counterpart to entropy.

Similar to while a person purchases a amazing pace of bandwidth for his or her Internet or Cell Phone issuer, one's Mind Manifestation System: the EEG Behavioral Spectrum within the Quantum Flux Spectrum of Consciousness, constantly and concurrently gives (at least) 5 varieties of informational and experiential "channels". However, alternatively of having to shop for them, you are born with those severa skills which is probably meant to be carried out and advanced.

Central to expertise this EEG Periodicity Learning Curve is that information gleaned from each thoughts bandwidth may be particular to the biology of that specific bandwidth in addition to essential to the individual's evolutionary diploma of analyzing.

For example, experiencing one's herbal, natural physical trance phenomenon in some unspecified time in the future of cushty wakefulness, someone is transitioning from neural oscillations taking place of their waking (beta) EEG Periodicity range (13-30 Hertz i.E.Thirteen-30 cycles in line with 2d) to the ones inside the (alpha) EEG Periodicity range (eight–12 Hertz i.E.

Eight-12cycles constant with 2d). Other EEG Periodicity levels are: delta (1–four Hz), and the "Shamanic" low gamma (30–70 Hz), and high gamma (70–one hundred fifty Hz) EEG Periodicity ranges. At four-8 Hz, theta mind waves stand up ultimately of deep meditation and slight sleep, collectively with the REM dream state.

The thoughts periodicities: collectively with Gamma (Super-Consciousness), Beta (Outer-Ego/Reasoning Mind), Alpha (Trance/Inner-Ego Mind), Theta (Dream/Inner-Ego Mind) and Delta (Deep Sleep-Coma/Inner Ego Mind), shape the organic organism called the mind: one's EEG physical mechanism's (EEG Behavioral Spectrum of Consciousness) supporting one's popular Quantum Flux Spectrum of Consciousness considering one's multidimensional participation within the extraordinary boom of recognition.

Information amongst linear Reality Framework One and nonlinear Reality Framework Two could likely normally flow had been it not for Outer-Ego's inherent censorship of nonlinear records from within Framework Two.

Indeed Outer-Ego's robust linear identification (related to its thirteen-30 Hertz bandwidth) separates waking awareness from its nonlinear Psychological Reality Frameworks of trance and dreams.

Compromised thru highbrow or physical trauma, this identity can harm down, permitting facts from the alternative Reality Frameworks to more really effect the Outer-Ego.

In terms of levels of private delight, it's no longer that the above Psychological Reality Frameworks' robotically provide more expansive reviews for a few and not others.

Having superior the potential to control power patterns among Reality Framework One and Two; thereby successfully engineering reality, the extra fulfilled man or woman knows that thoughts and their related feelings are vibration magnets able to be manipulated in infinitely lovable and innovative methods, just like the bricks and mortar of a physical shape.

In an entire lot the same way, goals integrate suitable devices and sports from All-That-Is into more enjoyable situations for the dreamer to actually include into waking truth.

Initially believing the subsequent dream to be an a laugh metaphor for my as an alternative doubtful house obligations skills, I fast discovered out it confirmed key factors of the dynamic device of interest. In the dream, I witnessed a vacuum purifier brimming with in recent times sucked-up dirt and debris (Integration of the Energy Levels of Consciousness), being cooked in a red-heat furnace (Amplification of the Energy Levels of Consciousness). The technique finished, a beautifully-fashioned cat emerged from that inferno. The dream demonstrates cognizance's innate integrations and amplifications of Focused Intent Energy Levels of Consciousness occurring among Framework Two and Framework One, influencing opportunity and final results.

Constantly exposed to numerous three-D experiential visible and audio-informational remarks, the Outer-Ego/Reasoning Mind always converts uncooked, sequential records from one's waking revel in. The degree of one's Hybrid Intellect/Emotionalism (the diploma of Framework Two's predominantly nonlinear organizational techniques blanketed into Framework One's predominantly linear organizational techniques), will determine the proportion of quantum intelligence introduced to the mix. This cooking/alchemic approach represents the Spiritualization of Matter wherein linear and/or nonlinear mind and emotions (as devices of consciousness) are long-established into waking fact thru recognition's innate integration/amplification techniques.

Modern physic's Entanglement and Superposition theories show the medium for all mind-to don't forget-strategies is notably talking nonlinear/simultaneous.

At its most sizeable level, Schrödinger's Cat Paradox represents the Wave Function of the Universe. Every particle inside the universe is ideally in a country of Superposition. In the Schrödinger's Cat metaphor, the cat is in an enclosed area and earlier than the sector is opened, the cat is in a country of

Superposition. This technique the cat can be belief of being simultaneously lifeless/alive: that because of the universe's innate nonlinearity, all states of being are as One. Opening the gateway for the multidimensionality of the All-That-Is Consciousness: all viable results of quantum measurements are physically located out in some realm or universe. The handiest way to determine the cat's actual state of being is to open the container. Once the sector is opened, the observer impact is immediately, inflicting the cat to have left the kingdom of Superposition. Therefore, the cat can be both dead or alive. In nature, all unobserved devices and activities are in a country of Superposition. When decided, they immediately input a way referred to as decoherence inflicting the wave to collapse into one country or each different this is then embedded interior its environment. As a remnant, the coherent thoughts united states is therefore translated as being in touch with the nonlinearity/simultaneity of desires.

According to the above paradox, then, thru looking at and deciphering your desires, you can stabilize, certainly show up, appropriate factors of the All-That-Is into waking fact. Awareness of and interplay with the contents of 1's dream worldwide, therefore, is one of the most direct strategies to keep away from default, complex waking realities. Able to define the form and color of the most complex concept paperwork, the advanced dreamer starts offevolved exploring facts commercial enterprise organization modalities typically unavailable to the Outer-Ego. Developing this form of mental functionality, one will become an adept inside the era of the manipulation of count number.

The one-of-a-kind profound mystery inside the lower back of Schrödinger's Cat and my dream cat having been let out of the bag is that each three-dimensional moment represents the functionality for all holographic ranges of being: the simultaneity of all realities gift inside the Quantum Flux Spectrum of Consciousness. While scientists are aware of the malleability of this Flux, it should be said that it's far human attention directing that malleability through the operational features of the Laws of Attraction, Consciousness Equilibrium and Consciousness's Quantum Fluctuations and their myriad outcomes.

It's an thrilling idea; that we've got got infinite possibilities inside the above Flux Spectrum to hone our hassle-fixing and manifestation capabilities. The multidimensionality of Selfhood motives non-public seasons to constantly be evolving someplace and in a few style. The question sincerely is: Do you need to consciously create your seasons of existence or do you need to passively standby as a few unlucky default season offers with you?

A most crucial way to treat waking-reality setbacks as opportunities for private growth is through consistent dream evaluation and journaling. Initiating this way, one ought to cultivate an intimate dating with their Reality

Framework Two; prioritizing useful beliefs and practical answers from the deepest a part of Self.

Such deep introspection can cause critical modifications in the layers of attention: Sometimes, we interpret a minute (a moment in time) constant with our temper. So, a second can be satisfied or frightened or it may include feelings of now not know-how what to do. It's good enough now not to recognize what to do. Just be with it. Just be with the reality that some factor that is actual one second isn't always actual, the following. There are many invested factors: factors that would effect the very last effects. Ultimately, the very last results depends upon the character's free will. Everyone desires to recognize the final results, the stop. However, there's no give up, nice "seasons of existence". We've all heard it said earlier than. Certain occasions, as an instance a circulate or a divorce, may be like a loss of life. There are other examples, of path. Rebirth, flowering, wizening and then dormancy: the springs, summers autumns and winters of our lives represent one's whole cycle of seasons. Karma is concerned in desire-making. There is a time to push and a time to allow pass. Everything in lifestyles is sort of a transport approach. A trouble may be like a starting: some element new may be crafted from an vintage problem. It's now not so critical approximately the stop or selection of a hassle, as an opportunity it is how you are with it; the way you engage with it. This 'birthing' is a gaining knowledge of gadget. This getting to know technique entails steady giving, studying, receiving, responding, interpreting and appreciating...Sadness is connected to all of this, humans now not looking to bear in thoughts in themselves. Yet, you constantly discover what you want.~ Kuan Yin

Indeed, you'll continually discover what you need in desires. In your waking truth, you possibly have responsibilities you experience or dislike. Beyond which can be areas of interest that you could no longer have developed however maintain a deep interest about. Offering opportunities for normal reinvention of oneself, goals will supply (regularly metaphorically), uncensored messages displaying the dreamer their relationship with their Original Grace: their innate mind-to-rely Law of Attraction dynamic for figuring out and attracting their most favored reality from myriad Probable Realities within the All That Is. Communicated as stories highlighting particular beliefs, feelings and tendencies in addition to delineating comparisons amongst one's waking and probably selves, goals elucidate the inspiration for all manifestation: that waking truth consequences are a cease end end result of 1's innermost desire.

Your in my view-engineered waking and dream truth recollections are based totally upon your philosophy of existence cultivated from memory variables from all recounted and unknown elements of the All-That-Is. Thus, waking and dream realities represent the dichotomy of 1's sequential specialty versus the greater/quantum revel in of who you're. Sometimes supplying uncomfortably candid reviews of the dreamer's waking truth, dreams display, (from the inner maximum part of self and without interference from Outer-Ego sequentially-based totally not unusual feel), the ideals/feelings chargeable for one's expansive or restricting waking fact.

Even more, they offer an endless reservoir of devices and occasions from one's Holographic Archives of Consciousness in which the expert dreamer can pick out that that lets in you to decorate their waking reality. Understanding the individual of one's dream gestalt is step one to initiate your dream evaluation and journaling protocols. Therefore, a outstanding characteristic of this e-book is delineation of the dream instructions that could comprise someone's dream gestalt. By defining: 1. Personalities, devices and activities within the dream. 2. The outstanding temper (s) of the dream. Three. Spoken messages within the dream, the dreamer has commenced out the method of turning into actively engaged with that which their dreams are searching for to relay.

Assisting the dreamer in defining personal agendas and the large parameters in their being, desires can also warn of probably events or offer glimpses of actual parallel realities. Thus, if a boogey guy arrives in your dream, it is probably clever to assess the ideals inside the decrease again of any fears you can despite the fact that own. Often showing superhuman possibly abilties, dreams can, but, open the dreamer's mind to possibilities well beyond what they will bear in mind themselves to be.

What are the underlying dynamics bearing in thoughts such complex private companies and interactions? Only pretty nowadays has the scientific situation of Computational Neuroscience began to remedy the mysteries of the brain's (as a minimum) five EEG Periodicities: the natural/intellectual bulwark comprising the Human EEG Behavioral Spectrum of Consciousness. Therefore, at the same time as it is proposed that occasions show up thru you; now not to you, it way (in contemporary mind-era terms) that each waking and non-waking event (which includes trance and goals) must be understood from the mind-set of the above complicated organizational/interplay device. And as in line with the Law of Attraction, that which you are, can be interested in you thru the feature of your innate Original Grace straddling the above-referred to Human EEG Behavioral Spectrum of Consciousness.

Vitality inner energy: waves inside waves!

What may be even more first-rate from the Outer-Ego's, linear mind-set is that the above organizational/interaction systems are parallel in nature. Similar to the relationship amongst a laptop and the Internet, there are automatic, simultaneous handshakes happening among one's Outer-Ego/Reasoning Mind's Reality Framework One and one's Inner-Ego/All-That-Is Mind's Reality Framework Two. And due to Reality

Framework Two's large thoughts/emotional organizational parameters, there can be recognizable and unrecognizable quantum handshake codecs associated with recognized and unknown objects, activities, intelligences and languages.

Computers are like savants, robotic marvels in positive choose out arenas. But they don't have emotions or instinct and the common experience of a five-year-vintage. On the possibility hand, humans automatically appoint complex and systematic approaches in which instructions found are blanketed again into the device this is being constructed. Thus a repressed, hidden part of self (consisting of a youngsters worrying incident) can impact one's gift-day reality.

While the majority of computer tactics are linear, a nonlinear idea can be identified thru many linear descriptions a good way to cumulatively describe that nonlinearity. As toward natural pc desirable judgment, there exist linear and nonlinear human EEG hassle-solving mechanisms suggesting that the thoughts is already primed for Law of Attraction mind-to-rely evolutions. For instance, in waking/linear mode, perception's and their emotions' affect inside the advent of personal truth can get away Outer-Ego's every day associative capabilities. Conversely, goals offer a nonlinear stage wherein beliefs and their feelings are played out as multidimensional, likely situations for the dreamer to potentially select from.

In the beyond, laptop systems solved troubles via very speedy calculations utilizing simplest one pathway. Today's Super Computer's hire parallel programming; infinite trouble-solving pathways to achieve a couple of feasible answers for a unmarried problem. Or, such complex programming ought to signify extra inexperienced strategies to pose a query for figuring out a sure final effects. Having a couple of trouble-fixing modes (collectively with waking, trance and dream Psychological Reality Frameworks), the human thoughts can not, although, be as compared to any present or destiny pc.

Beginning to stagnate in a unmarried's every day existence, one have to experience a dream take-heed call from their Inner Ego. Thus, you may experience incredible insights inside the route of an everyday dream or an superb daydream or hypnotic trance at some point of an in any other case regular day. A huge sea of records and trouble-solving equipment, the latent actualization pool of All-That-Is awaits the curtain—the sequential veil of waking fact, to rise.

Chapter 3: The Universal Laws of Attraction

The Law of Attraction states: The diploma to that you take transport of/love yourself is probably contemplated in all that is interested in you. Intimately related with the above significant law, yet mainly related to the organizational stability amongst Psychological Reality Framework One and Two, The Law of Consciousness Equilibrium states: The Dynamic System of Consciousness has a consistent, propensity inside the direction of balancing the physical, emotional and religious rate weather between Framework One and Two, thereby presenting stabilizing, expansive answers vital to the survival/evolution of the dreamer.

Computers at the least in part resemble human attention's operational structures concerning the above Psychological Reality Frameworks One and Two. Whereas reminiscence in human interest is innate, any laptop want to be instructed on what it's far and the way to act (at each boot-up) by way of Read Only Memory (ROM). Having infinitely a ways more ability to preserve memory then any device, the All-That-Is, as critical to the human dynamic device of reputation, harbors and sustains all reminiscences having ever existed.

The combining of popularity's dynamic tool with the Law of Attraction effects in steady small and large adjustments taking place among Psychological Reality Framework's One and Two for the functions of mastering and balance. Whereas gravity is the stabilizer for the body and exceptional bodily structures, the dynamic machine of awareness, walking in tandem with the Law of Attraction, is the stabilizer and sustainer of memories due to the fact the catalysts for the advent of reality.

Were it now not for its capacity to dream—to mechanically access Psychological Reality Framework Two, despite the fact that, humanity would possibly in no manner be introduced to best, trade reminiscences locked inside the vault of All-That-Is. My series of Chalice desires, as an example, were metaphors showing that what one chooses to keep in mind, forms their reality. Similarly, the mala bead, diamond and pearl necklace retrieved from my dream vault (Chapter 5C), turned into a metaphor for expansive recollections to be retrieved from one's All-That-Is. Conversely, my dream, wherein I turn out to be capable of magically penetrate my hand through a glass pane, confirmed that the second one I doubted my capability to get admission to the treasure trove of All-That-Is, the glass solidified and I modified into now not allowed front.

Messengers of first-rate memories dwelling within the All-That-Is, goals offer an exchange, best tale to replace one's possibly unbeneficial waking tale. For example, a person has been, for awhile, experiencing a darkish duration in their waking truth. In dreams, they will discover themselves as residing a fulfilling and completely satisfied life. Giving validation to the type of tremendous tale and then placing in advance it in some unspecified time in the future of waking truth, the character is using interest's built-in buffer closer to any perceived chaos. Thus, Reality Framework Two is specially designed to provide expansive, change reminiscences for Reality Framework One to affirm and ultimately entice.

Within the Mind Probabilities/Frequencies/Manifestation System, each Evolutionary Level of Learning and its holographic imprints, will lure similarly-enlightened know-how and evaluations. Dramatic elevations of 1's parallel fact charge climates will concurrently have an effect on dreams and one's complete gestalt of consciousness. Individuals vibrating inside the higher degrees of getting to know frequency tiers will attraction to matching higher frequency-ranges of studying thru goals and during waking truth.

When dreaming, therefore, you've got the capacity to recognize the countless scope of your being. However, as the species pursuit of effective manipulation of be counted range could require the improvement of discrimination, Outer-Ego's easy and complex differentiating strategies reason it to continuously attempt to categorize out of doors and inner information inner its particularly slender linear, perceptual bandwidth.

As is typically stated, the thoughts is lots extra than the measurable anatomy and phenomena related to the mind. As the EEG Periodicity Spectrum can not be characterised as surely empirical, to in reality understand the scope of human interest is to accept Outer-Ego's dating with the Inner-Ego. That coma patients were documented to show off simply new personalities upon awakening, suggests that after the person is biking within the slower EEG stages of popularity (with dwindled Outer-Ego/Reality Framework One input), they interface with ultimate portions of the general Self's saved reminiscences and possibly selves. Thus, in contrast to a laptop dropping all capability to maintain its RAM even as powered off, the All-That-Is is recognition's everlasting, overarching, innate and dynamic storage and sustainer of reminiscences.

Indeed, to bear in mind the thoughts, body and soul perform in a separate and haphazard fashion is to accept as true with we haven't any control over reality. And at the same time as it's far my motive to offer as many examples as viable concerning the validity of parallel communications/interactions amongst Reality Framework One and Two, possibly the maximum profound evidence can be located in the following goals:

Dozing off right right into a half-sleep one middle of the night I changed into aware, for a cut up second, of straddling parallel worlds. While repositioning my bodily legs right into a extra cushty function, I abruptly sensed a few one of a kind pair of legs, now not of this waking reality but despite the fact that real, spontaneously reposition themselves. In a comparable dream-twilight incident, I felt someone or some issue, from the opportunity element, touching me!

Another example of popularity simultaneously-straddling one's waking and dream worlds (Reality Framework One and Two) confirmed my accomplice, John and I consoling a nervous and hungry Syrian war orphan. Comforting the younger boy; telling him that most effective the body dies and that the soul lives on in myriad parallel existences, I realized the kid's facial capabilities, no matter the fact that framed by the use of darkish hair (John's hair is blond) reflected the ones of John's and that he became one among John's parallel selves! Serendipitously, at that very 2nd, I come to be conscious, from my half-sleep, of John mulling in the course of the kitchen and the sound of the microwave heating water for his tea.

Indeed, hypnosis customers have relayed their reviews of this twin recognition; of attempting, from their goals, to capture the attention of someone meandering about in their waking fact.

Humans incarnate to earth aware of the evaluation—the combination of activities and consciousnesses they'll be immersed in—knowing it is the catalyst; pushing them to redefine their private manifestation-expertise barriers. All the at the identical time as, absolutely everyone holds, internal themselves, the memory of the better interest geographical areas serving because the axiom for all cultural comparisons. And whilst occasions taking place round you may seem as continuously shifting, you may rest within the truth that your Inner Integrity—your Soul Core Essence can not be corrupted through the usage of any outdoor effect and anything you reputation upon will ultimately shape your reality.

Here on this planet, one has an opportunity to conform their specialty and creativity within the flesh; their dating with their Original Grace. True pragmatism, therefore, is the knowledge that personal perceptions can adjust that this is fabric—that this magical technique is, definitely, the sensible technique to life.

The Outer-Ego/Reasoning Mind is so carefully aligned with written and spoken metaphor associated with sequential time that it is straightforward to continuously slip outside and inside of a metaphorical united states of america; hypnotized with the useful resource of their private thoughts or conversations with others. Recall how many cultural sayings reflect the notion in sequential time: time is cash, biding my time, time is on my difficulty, over and over, now may be the time, in no manner enough time, time is of the essence, subsequent time, all of the time in the international or out of time.

And instead of mere figures of speech, those metaphors represent deeply-imbedded Outer-Ego organizational conventions influencing humanity's waking fact. Woven collectively, everyday sayings create a linear metaphorical map of methods we understand ourselves inside the Linear-Thought-Construct Medium of waking truth. Objects and sports will then fill inside the ones maps; long lasting linear agendas wherein parallel techniques although arise. Within every spoken word or sung phrase, therefore, there are parallel pulsations. Thus, even inner obvious linear time, there may be nonlinear idea-constructs.

In dreams, nonlinear metaphor supersedes linear metaphor to create its very very own wonky organizational conventions: perceptions and/or interactions. Therefore, one also can want to enjoy an intimate interest of the form and color of a legitimate. They could possibly experience the intensity of their inner mild or robotically recognize and talk some historical, unknown dialect.

Determined to defend itself from the otherness of nonlinear statistics, in spite of the fact that, the Outer-Ego/Reasoning Mind has a brilliant capability to turn out to be recalcitrant; rejecting out of hand any of what it considers to be internal/alien facts. When there may be turmoil; while the veil of waking fact is finally lifted, there may be bleed-via of exchange statistics from the Inner-Self, thereby stimulating an acceleration of reputation. These Inner Ego intrusions on the way to try to subvert linear concept-construct blockages shaped through way of Outer Ego's slim perceptions:

Listen to the oneness:

the roar and the silence!

Wind and sea!

You and me!

Waves internal waves.

Becoming and be!

Chapter 4: Dream Allegory, Archetypes, Artifacts and Alchemy

You want to taste those types of research. And the Outer-Ego makes it possible. Don't curse the ego. So many scriptures curse the ego self. Instead, regard your existence as approximately alternatives, research and choice and which you are already liberated. Don't be fearful of choice.

It is why you're right here: to flavor, stay. It's truly an 'agreement' you all made at the same time as you took on an ego. You splintered off from the whole. ~ Kuan Yin

The tumultuous political activities of the nineteen-sixties marked the start of a trendy era of interest—that humanity might often cross decrease returned from Outer-Ego's linear "otherness" to its extra inclusive, unique country of the All-That-Is. That humanity had fulfilled integration and amplification of its linearly-received Creative Force organizational abilties intended an acceleration of the Hybrid Intellect/Emotionalism: prolonged inclusion of Framework Two nonlinear information into Framework One.

Thus, enhancement of dream fee, awesome and depth might in all likelihood, an increasing number of, alter the person of risk and very last outcomes for the entire species' waking truth.

Because of the above said quickening, lots of my readers for the time being are likely discovering the stability handiest dream archetypes can offer. Involved in the species' move lower again from Outer-Ego's instead slim, linear attitude to regularly nonlinear states of focus, individuals might also experience, as have I, archetypal desires having, as an example, the Chalice, the Tree of Life, the Cosmic Fabric, the Inner Light and Sound, the Cosmic Lute, the Pool of

Consciousness, Gods and Goddesses, and plenty of others. As their critical dream challenge. Additionally, they will, increasingly more, enjoy lucid, premonition, psychic circle of relatives, superhuman, and so on. And mainly manipulation of count number desires as popularity of the power inner advances.

In desires, (as synthesizers of the divine alignment amongst Reality Frameworks One and Two) there can be a blending of every archetype and artifact. Whereas Outer-Ego/Reasoning Mind lets in for the capacity and evolution of one's specific and current artifacts, Inner-Ego/All-That-Is Mind maintains the genuine archetypes even as deciding on from Reality Framework One's cultural norms and artifacts, new archetypes.

As they exemplify humanity's majestic transformative potentials in an increasingly more chaotic international, effective historic and current artifical creations, along with the Mona Lisa, Pablo Picasso's, Nude Descending a Staircase, and Impressionist Works collectively with Vincent Van Gogh's, Starry Night and Claude Monet's Lilies, further to classical to modern composer's works expressing chaos and determination, have finished archetypal reputation. Because of such immoderate ranking, they've been included into the Collective Unconsciousness Creation Gestalt. For this purpose, you can thoroughly experience such works as key talents of your dream.

There are other dream indicators of the transformational generation we're now in. For example, you could, as have I, envision your self in dreams as a form of messenger among worlds. Such a dream may be symbolic for the above-noted retrieval of Framework One's progressive achievements into the All-That-Is and/or inclusion of Framework Two's expansive, nonlinear statistics into Framework One:

In my dream, I observed myself and my grandsons standing at the sea floor and defensive hands. From time to time, I should swim to the surface, reputedly reporting their records and moreover retrieving records to be taken lower lower again and shared with my grandsons. Naturally, the bottom of the sea represents the sizeable, nonlinear reserve of Framework Two records on the same time because the ground is symbolic for Framework One's waking fact, linear information. Symbolic for the transfer of nonlinear to linear records and vice versa, the dream elucidated the Dynamic System of Consciousness incremental to the enlargement of cognizance.

Now, it may seem farfetched to indicate that the atom bomb has been raised, for higher or worse, to archetypal recognition. Yet, cultural myths abound with memories of gods and goddesses having the electricity of introduction and destruction of worlds.

Assuming this fact is what Kuan Yin purports it to be: that sure energies are "not as effective" and consequently have incarnated in the global "to growth in recognition and energy", the subsequent quote from Oracle of Compassion: the Living Word of Kuan Yin, reveals why I advise that the atom bomb is emblematic for overdevelopment of Outer-Ego awareness: that mankind's simultaneous bellicosity/invincibility, (that an man or woman is time and again reborn through reincarnation), has done archetypal recognition:

I don't truely understand what I'm seeing. I certainly see many shapes and forms of Kuan Yin," keeps Lena. Now I'm witnessing a scene of Hiroshima, a outstanding mushroom cloud. She's inner it. Now it's miles indoors of her. Suddenly, it explodes in her frame and she or he absorbs, becomes the electricity. That's her message for this financial disaster. Nothing can harm Her. Even the most devastating stress is changed, softened in order that human beings will broaden even when experiencing complete destruction. She's no longer afraid to merge with the maximum fearsome creations."

"You see," proclaims Kuan Yin, "I am but in my actual form. It didn't spoil me!"

According to Kuan Yin, it is our duty to Imagine the opportunities of something more than is proper proper right here. The electromagnetic layers of mild and sound can, from expansive or proscribing beliefs, coalesce into their related holographic archetypal formations. Individuals in the end appeal to their archetypes. Indeed, Kuan Yin, because the archetype of loving-kindness is so powerful that She can fall apart the darkest of energies.

As the interaction most of the archetypal electricity groupings is synergistic, they'll spontaneously enchantment to matching truth-parameters. While not an archetype, the Fear Triad is an instance of the way terrible, spherical ideals can with out end volley from side to side, from time to time for lifetimes, without choice. And as humanity can in no way be in reality freed from its innate goals, guilt for having choice is one of the principal attractors of unwanted realities.

Naturally, ideals and intentions of loving kindness and generosity additionally give a boost to every exceptional. Possessing inbuilt treatments for any stagnation, humanity periodically attracts Cosmic Speakers informing us of our inherent Law of Attraction, Consciousness Equilibrium and Consciousness Quantum Fluctuation inherent forces. Ultimately, love, satisfaction and gratitude set the vibration for the abundance that follows!

Falling into shut eye, I as quickly as dreamt I become on a totally small island with amazing human beings. One of the humans I diagnosed as my mother. I couldn't, even though, decide the alternative man or woman's face. Rapidly walking out of meals and water, our little organization became, minute thru minute, turning into an increasing number of involved. We knew with out a few decisive movement, we had no risk of surviving an lousy lot longer. The high-quality break out, I reasoned, may be to dive into the huge, ominous waves; swimming out into the transport lane in hopes a passing freighter may rescue us. Then, I witnessed myself dive into the ocean waves (Framework Two), even as mom and the mystery individual fearfully huddled collectively at the shore (Reality Framework One), contemplating their future.

Once conscious, I attempted to determine this profound symbolism; that humanity is dropped into this worldwide: this small island bandwidth of waking reality's Framework One whilst having Framework Two's expansive opportunities simplest a dream away. Immediately confronted with the mystery of existence and survival; our recollections in huge component erased through cycles of delivery and rebirth, we're left with the amazing preference; we could courageously dive into the unknown, multidimensional ocean of Framework Two? Or shall we stay stranded in this archipelago of truth; confined through Outer-Ego's as an alternative solitary statistics of itself?

Further reading the dream, I knew my diving into the waves come to be metaphorical for my unwavering interest in linear as opposed to nonlinear organizational/interaction capabilities in Reality Framework One and Two; that the human intellectual EEG waves forming the Quantum Flux Spectrum of Consciousness are crucial to the advent of reality.

Were it now not for trance and goals and recollections of some difficulty even grander than our waking existence, we might forever pick to validate best that facts gleaned from the highbrow island of Outer-Ego's pretty-confined stage of mastering:

Chapter 5: Differentiating Archetype/Artifact Energy Pattern Dreams

Prioritizing for its very very very own survival the Outer-Ego/Reasoning Mind utilizes its sequential organizational abilities to set up the relevance and desirability of every of waking lifestyles's objects and sports. In its reflected photo of sequential personal and social reviews, Outer Ego's perceptions have end up sequentially-diagnosed and metaphorical. Conversely, in its pondered image of nonlinear studies, the Inner-Ego's perceptions have become nonlinearly identified and metaphorical.

When dreaming, therefore, one may be confronted with archetypal and artifact dream troubles furnished in a nonlinear metaphorical layout apparently quite distorted from waking mind's sequential metaphorical format. Which the actual distortion? One can also additionally ask.

In its spontaneous procurement of the top notch trove of gadgets and sports dwelling within the All-That-Is, Inner-Ego will make use of its dream pallet of allegory, archetypes and artifacts; colorizing and occasionally even reverberating private electricity patterns on its top notch dream canvas. Some clean, some murky, colours and sounds function metaphors for private waking lifestyles notion choices. In desires, you may sincerely consequently witness a single concept or emotion morphing into symbolic formations in no way anticipated by using way of the Outer Ego.

Various cultures in the course of the a while felt the want to particular the universality of nature as deeply mental and/or non secular bodily artifacts. The Mandala of Buddhism, the Double Triangle of Judaism, the Yin-Yang of Taoism, the Chalice, the Tree of Life, advantageous musical gadgets which consist of the lute, flute and harp, and the Serpent are however samplings of the hybrid nature/artifical, archetypes/artifacts symbolizing the endless elements of your All-That-Is as expressed in goals. For instance, the archetype of the circulate, in many cultures, represents the four factors of the arena (earth, air, water, fireside), uniting at the middle. These 4 elements regularly take vicinity in dreams as symbols for personality dispositions and electricity styles. As may be demonstrated, the majority of desires delineated herein have archetypal topics. One even includes the Archetypal Fabric (the sum ordinary of all archetypes).

Indeed, the All-The-Is typically delights within the range composing its very Oneness. Thus, the Great Expansion of Consciousness is superior through each unique expression of Self on the equal time as even though very last part of the whole. Carl Gustav Jung's seminal work delineating the archetypes establishes that gadgets and sports activities inside the psyche are crucial and resilient in the Collective Unconscious. Endlessly shifting thru the generations like water in a few winding go together with the float, they are the serpent of interest.

Because of the simultaneity of the Law of Consciousness Quantum Fluctuations, but, this manuscript discourages any presumption of duality, thereby unifying Jung's initially-separate archetypes. Thus, I've mixed animus/anima, delivery/loss of life, introduction/destruction, mom/father/infant, statistics/anger/pride, chaos/stability, and masses of others. As patterns of power: the entwined/juxtaposed archetypal symbols occupying their particular positions within the gestalt of interest.

An instance of an entwined/juxtaposed dream archetype and its corresponding strength pattern is the "outcast author"—a distorted model of its cousin: the right, all-powerful Creative Self. As the tale of this dream archetype is one story of humanity's adventure of rejection and reclamation of its innate electricity to create reality referred to for the duration of the dream gestalt, the outcast creator/all-effective Creative Self entwined/juxtaposed archetype represents a specific power sample of chaos and backbone within the Great Expansion of Consciousness.

Because of the universality of the entwined/juxtaposed dream archetypes, Outer Ego can't subdue those symbols not unusual to all humanity. Nor, can it save you unconscious expression of dream artifacts moreover living interior one's depths of interest. In artifact goals, then, one also can additionally find out historic artifacts from one or greater era's informing the dreamer they are persisting in an antiquated thoughts-set that now not serves them. Indeed, automobiles, planes and brilliant motors from modern-day or past eras, can feature metaphors for occasions dominating a specific historic length and the beliefs behind it. To refine your dream evaluation and journaling skills, pay attention to the uniforms or costumes supplied within the dream further to a few different historic artifacts, consisting of furniture, music played or languages spoken.

Accurate interpretation will depend upon the dreamer's excellent or horrible association with the particular dream item/event. As with archetypal desires, notwithstanding the fact that, artifact goals can involve gadgets, activities and eras no longer right away recognizable to the dreamer, perhaps indicating the dreamer's participation in a few however to be actualized fact.

There are also what is probably termed supernatural archetype and artifact desires; inanimate devices all of sudden turning into animate: an object simultaneously manifesting as an event! Thus, as instructed in Oracle of Compassion: the Living Word of Kuan Yin, my customer, Lena Lees, observed sooner or later of trance, deity Kuan Yin draw upon her big repertoire of archetypes demonstrating the plasticity of the soul. Beautiful more youthful maiden, mother or wizened crone! Death and rebirth! Undulating rock formations and fathomless galaxies! They had been but samplings of Her clever and boundless transformational powers; her mind-increasing metamorphisms showed the multidimensional mosaic of interest.

Kuan Yin symbolizes the divine expression of be counted range variety and energy. The embodiment of the nature of the universe as it in reality exists while Outer-Ego sequential selection is eliminated, She represents every in all likelihood arrangement of elemental constructing blocks. Deriving Her strength from the Quantum Fluctuations, She office paintings first-rate and infinitesimal self-creations from ranges of scale large and small.

Offering vibration pathways inside the path of healing, the eternal forming and reforming of personal archetypal and artifact electricity patterns stay in accordance with non-public beliefs. An instance is probably that someplace alongside the manner, love and passion has turn out to be associated with grief and warfare, thereby forming its distorted archetypal electricity pattern. True dream alchemy, in this case, might comprise converting the above proscribing belief with expansive establishments regarding love and passion, thereby reforming private power patterns: vistas of 1's but unrealized portions of Self:

Initially no longer conscious this have become an energy pattern dream, I as soon as witnessed severa, probably ten, vortices (like spinning hands) protruding from my frame. Rotating in a counter-clockwise fashion, with out be aware, they may all, in unison with my heart/breath (Prāṇa) pulse, exchange direction, thereby redefining the effulgence/vibration field surrounding and radiating out from me.

In a related power-pattern dream, I got here upon the daunting sight of burnt-out ruins; only the concrete slab of this as quickly as sound building nonetheless remained. Scrutinizing the encompassing grounds, I located that converting what have to have been gravestones had been five distinct mandala styles. Realizing these had been strength styles seemingly defining the essence of every of the deceased, I understood that an individual's archetypal power sample will observe them from bodily into nonphysical life.

It is inside the countless, timeless ocean of Psychological Reality Framework Two, then, that the holographic realities, like waves, will shape and reform: building into towering monuments or absolutely washing away. Maintain religion that in spite of apparent human frailties and foibles, we are a resilient species and there are limitless opportunities inside a quantum universe to take place our highest dreams. The right definition of recovery, therefore, is that deliberate alteration of your archetypal strength patterns is to change the vibration you offer to the universe which you can, in flip, attraction to: It's a dream. Remember? You're living a dream. It's very complex to keep the dream and live the dream. You are gaining knowledge of the art of juggling the dream and the arena of goals. Nobody really receives harm.~ Kuan Yin

Dream dynamics will faithfully reflect ideas of the acquainted Laws of Attraction, Consciousness Equilibrium and Consciousness Quantum Fluctuations. One or more of the subsequent Fifteen Universal Law Dynamics can display themselves inside the Sixteen Dream Classifications:

1. Quantum Fluctuations and the multidimensional tiers of being.

2. Objects and activities of the All-That-Is.

three. That apparent chaos precedes order.

4. The eternal integrity of the soul.

5. Archetypal strength styles.

6. The Original Grace go with the flow between Reality Framework One and Two.

7. Consciousness Atmospherics: area-time behaving in every different way within the various parallel realities.

eight. Beliefs and their corresponding emotions.

nine. The remoted ego instead of All-That-Is and retrieval of the repressed self.

10. The holographic universe.

11. The human/nature connection.

12. The inner moderate of liberation and internal sound of don't forget.

13. Dream alchemy.

14. The Spiritualization of Matter.

15. Immediate instead of perceived delayed actualization of gadgets and sports.

Chapter 6: Hybrid Intellect/Emotionalism

Most regard the thoughts in terms of Outer Ego's linear "beta cognizance", wherein movements and reactions are skilled inside the linear context of waking truth. As a hypnotherapist, I'm aware about different kinds of mind collectively with the Inner-Ego's alpha and theta nonlinear interest as nicely the thoughts of the physical body—what is known as "cell reminiscence". Possessing its very own attention; a complex community of regarded and unknown waking and non-waking psychic/physical body moves and reactions, cell memory also can display itself as messages in trance or desires or as abreactions in waking fact.

Scientists, psychologists and psychiatrists have lengthy referred to there had been as a minimum 3 awesome mind behaviors: waking, trance and sleep. Only pretty presently, however, had been scientists able to understand at least 5 extremely good thoughts-wave oscillation stages (or EEG periodicities) and their related human behaviors. Empirical facts about those awesome stages now affords a template for thoughts waves and their corresponding behaviors.

Behaviors inside the amazing-recognition (gamma), waking (beta) trance (alpha) and sleep (theta) and ultra-slow (delta) agencies may be referenced as gamma, beta, alpha, theta and delta behaviors, respectively. For the functions of this manuscript, behaviors related to waking reality (for example talking, reasoning, giggling, weeping and bodily motion) are usually grouped as "beta behavior".

Envisioning, abreactions, cataleptic reactions, heightened targeted hobby and suggestibility are commonly categorised beneath "alpha conduct". REM and specific dream and sleep-associated behaviors are predominantly grouped beneath "theta" and/or "delta behavior". There are also unique styles of indicators and one-of-a-type opportunity behaviors associated with the extraordinary-aware and the extremely-gradual EEG waves. These represent the specific expressions professional at the acute polarities of the human spectrum of focus.

EEG behaviors are critical to specific mind approaches effecting the fitness and stability of our complicated physiological and intellectual systems. As stated, the two primary perceptual modalities: Outer-Ego's linear and Inner-Ego's nonlinear pulses, dictate how the entity will interpret their outer and inner environments, respectively.

They're additionally inherent to the various strength levels of focus within the Quantum Flux Spectrum of Consciousness, concerning opportunity and very last consequences.

The time period, Serpent Intellect—what I later decided out had been latent, intellectual tactics residing inside the very depths of cognizance, have turn out to be at the begin introduced to me on the same time as awakening from a dream. My curiosity peaked, I concerned myself inside the study of historic literature describing the numerous serpent symbols. Whereas the ouroboros or uroborus depicts a serpent or dragon ingesting its very very personal tail and is symbolic for disambiguation, the yin/yang with its black and white halves is the Chinese photograph for advent. Another which means that that for the ancient spiral photo is that it represents attention starting from its center and growing outwardly. The Tibetan Kalachakra, sometimes presenting concentric circles (much like the CMB temperature variant concentric earrings), or worlds indoors worlds, shows this information has constantly been to be had to mankind. Crop Circles additionally often feature a concentric circle motif. There is likewise every other opportunity: that the concentric circles mirror the layered holographic realities encountered in desires.

From the above research plus additional intuitive statistics, I've decided that the Serpent Intellect is, in formation and actualization, much like the ouroboros.

Representing the simultaneity of a concept-form within the path of the holographic power ranges of popularity, not anything separates its have an effect on due to the fact the serpent's head and tail are one.

You may probable regard the Serpent Intellect as you may a snake inside the wild. Having exquisite formations: the wavy (Integration/Quantum Channel) line and the coiled (Amplifier/Quantum Channel) line, the ones formations are repeated all through the whole thing of nature, as an instance: the wavy jet drift and the storm/twister tightly-coiled vortices.

However, due to the simultaneity of the universe, the wavy and coiled strains are definitely superimposed—top notch-positioned! In terms of time and no-time (linearity and nonlinearity), for instance, they constitute the oneness of noun and verb: i.E. The acquired/obtaining, the sought/trying to find. And due to the continuing Great Expansion of Consciousness, the as quickly as separate/chaotic Energy Levels of Consciousness will, via integration and amplification, in the end evolve once more to their unique country of oneness.

Currently, there's a exceptional deal of interest in Predictive Analytics: the Informational Age's scientific quest regarding possibility and very last outcomes. In a completely linear universe, devoid of the observer effect, a sequential mapping of possibility and very last consequences may make ideal revel in. However, because of the multidimensional implications of the observer impact, there may be a couple of possible consequences and the future continuously creates the beyond.

In terms of popularity, the best determinant for predictability, then, is the Serpent Intellect: that a belief-shape in a single realm has durability in all others. As our species is presently involved in accelerating its degree of psychic equilibrium between Reality Framework One and Two, this quickening: this boom of consciousness, calls for that Outer-Ego's, Reality Framework One's as an alternative slender bandwidth be substantially increased. Through recording of 1's goals, as an example, the character is straight away acknowledging their involvement with Reality Framework Two.

With endurance, this courting amongst Framework One and Two can expand, causing step by step more colourful dreams that would evolve into deeply meaningful communications. Actively engaged in this method, one eventually will growth levels of Reality Framework Two's nonlinear statistics into Reality Framework One. Steady integration and amplification of this deeper focus: i.E. The Serpent Intellect, will create evolutionary shifts the least bit degrees of recognition bearing in thoughts equilibrium most of the two frameworks ensuing in skillful manipulation of depend. Unfortunately, a continual predominance of (especially proscribing) linear information in Reality

Framework One, can create the same old complex, default realities.

While Outer-Ego's sequential-oriented beta pulse is regarded as this civilization's reputable hobby medium, without the Laws of Attraction, Consciousness Equilibrium and Consciousness Quantum Flux philosophies, a society is bereft of its in-constructed system for gaining the deeply-enticing views vital for its very own growth of popularity. Chronically dismissing messages from their dreams; labeling them as invalid and probably even corruptive, an individual must enjoy dream bleed-via: Framework Two messages encouraging Outer-Ego's lively engagement with one's internal information. If those messages are continuously ignored, the dreamer may additionally in the end enjoy what I term as a Physical Impact Dream: Framework Two-induced bodily sensations and reactions.

Reality Framework Two encompasses endless ranges of reading interior an ever-increasing universe imagined to be protected and amplified for acceleration of 1's waking revel in. Knowledge equals strength. As one's thoughts is perfectly-advanced to glean know-how from their Framework Two, levels of expertise derived from therein after which covered into one's waking revel in will, to that specific diploma, increase one's Energy/Knowledge Quotient.

There are the nested holographic layers from which private intentions upward push up in the shape of concept and emotional impulses: the the use of forces for the advent of reality. Reality Framework Two offers a nonlinear popularity, releasing the dreamer from waking-reality linear constraints, in which decision of any limiting notion/emotion is viable. Possessing multidimensional staging regions, dreams provide intimate intellectual frontiers for development of nonlinear know-how in volition and focus.

The quantum element of private truth is that we each represent a particular grouping of atoms an amazing way to simultaneously reproduction itself with versions. Naturally, this means countless self-factors to choose from. The mind, terms and feelings you challenge (as they're actual extensions of you), will red meat up or negate your real atomic form. One's unfastened will to pick out out out idea/emotion projections has profound implications for evolving the Outer-Ego; that when awakening to each new dawn, it has the possibility to create expansive, new realities.

Integral to mind-to-depend manifestation strategies, integrating and amplification of linear and nonlinear data occurring in Reality Framework One and Two is the number one differentiating element among human evolution and different species. Whereas other species keep to specialize of their unique regions, organic, quantum Informational Dynamics taking place among the Reality Frameworks permit for evolution of the complexities within the Human EEG Spectrum of Consciousness: i.E. The Quantum

Flux Spectrum of Consciousness. As love and worry are the number one appeal forces for any item or event; their mind/emotional resonances, blended with aware affirmations, create powerful attraction elements simultaneously expanding or contracting all levels of cognizance.

It's thrilling to evaluate the mechanics and techniques of a laptop image application with the above For instance, on every occasion one clicks the computer mouse, that motion is considered an 'event'. If one clicks the mouse on a wonderful task panel and creates, as an instance, a exact circle, the circle is taken into consideration an 'item'. Whether one creates a totally tough circle or absolutely deletes it, the circle becomes part of the picture software software (i.E. The Quantum Flux Spectrum of Consciousness).

Continuing with the same circle object instance, viable command the laptop to dim or spotlight a high-quality percent of that equal circle item. To accumulate a particular seen quit end result, one may additionally need to layer a square over or underneath the circle. Adding more layers, one has created a queue of vertically stacked layers. He/she may then need to supply a sample to the again of the queue and bring some other sample to the foreground for a extra practical effect.

Moreover, gadgets in a layout can become distorted, mutated or nearly unrecognizable with every improvement of clicks on the 'effects' buttons. Occasionally an unwanted part of an item could likely peek via the layers, spoiling the complete effect of the layout. To alleviate the unwanted detail, the artist should sift thru the queue, deleting the layer containing the undesired object.

Now, you can probably apprehend why the layers in a laptop-programming queue is probably in evaluation to the development of your Hybrid Intellect/Emotionalism. There is, but, an vital distinction. When truely uploading nonlinear records from Framework

Two to One, you're growing a vibrational shift within the Quantum Flux Spectrum of Consciousness:

The point isn't to drag the terrible past or destiny into the existing. Understanding the opportunities of the prevailing! It's a potential beneficial for discovering the divine. You slip into the universe, even as residing in this dream, this gift. Your break out hatch is proper proper here. I need you to experience the most divine lifestyles possible. Thoughts can effect the way the location can go. What an extensive concept! Everyone having loving kindness! With exercise, a truth is created somewhere having that very interest of loving kindness. Such exercise furthermore attracts one to those loving kindness planes of interest. ~ Kuan Yin

The resonance of affection, compassion and recognition contrasts dramatically with the resonance of blame and anger. Similar to particle pulsations transferring internal and out of lifestyles, remarkable or dim enchantment factors constitute integration and amplification of the numerous power levels of cognizance within the Quantum Flux Spectrum of Consciousness. When those vibrations engage, bodily and highbrow responses acquire and are recorded within the mobile memory. It is that this non-forestall coalescing and dispersing of energy figuring out risk and outcome. You in the long run draw out of your Quantum Flux Spectrum of Consciousness into waking truth simplest that which you vibrate with. Like the sidewinder snake; its frame following the pinnacle (i.E. The thoughts) in rhythmic undulation, it's miles personal ideals/emotions which can be the attractors.

Similar to excellent species in nature, in spite of the fact that destroy unfastened humanity's required planned manipulation of groups amongst Framework One and Two, the cellular memory possesses its very private inherently-balanced Hybrid Intellect/Emotionalism: focus of its simultaneous participation within the

Quantum Flux Spectrum of Consciousness. When Outer-Ego will become overly compromised with the aid of the rigors and tribulations of waking truth, the cellular reminiscence will regularly, in the shape of trance or dream messaging, try to reset the stability amongst Framework One and Two. Thus, following a day of excessive linearly-stimulated highbrow/emotional input, a person also can dream of floating in a galaxy or some other shape of thoughts-expanding revel in.

Reality is the opportunity of what's often assumed. Time and place do not provide a window wherein human reputation is completed out. Instead, powerful convergences of ideals and feelings create domestic home windows of possibility inner Quantum Fluctuations. Articulating a 2nd is consequently described as projected beliefs forming replicate Psychological Reality Frameworks—duplicate attention home windows of opportunity that could, in turn, upload momentum to the triumphing 2d.

The adaptability of the Quantum Flux Spectrum of Consciousness: its functionality to routinely reorganize sequential and quantum information from the 2 Psychological Reality Frameworks, is critical for the Outer-Ego's a hit navigation of the worrying situations of modern-day waking truth. Historically, Shamans have applied Framework Two's more-sensory facts for tribal cultural protection. Generally talking, this spectrum's traditional evolutions have employed Outer-Ego's sequential perceptions and groups for development of focused reason. The byproduct of this necessity may additionally want to necessarily comprise transient restraint of Inner-Ego's stepped forward perceptions.

Obviously, the degree of cooperation and/or war stemming from the sequential/quantum informational/emotional natures of Framework One and Two will determine the intensity, outstanding and price of ongoing Psychic Informational Dynamics of Consciousness on individual and mass reality.

It therefore behooves the Outer-Ego to be greater open to the exquisite, quantum facts originating in Framework Two. The percent of one's Hybrid Intellect/Emotionalism (the proportion of Framework Two's expansive records included into Framework One), will determine the character's degree of non-distorted perceptions.

And at the same time as your waking fact also can seem chaotic, take comfort that one's Inner Value Climate of Psychological Reality (one's Inner-Self Integrity), is the for all time cross-to for stability/equilibrium.

A maximum critical importance of Kuan Yin's imaginitive changes is that they may be metaphors for the private transformation of notion into rely. Her following windsurfer parable emphasizes the significance of focusing on handiest that which you want to gain—how proper Focused Intent can assist one efficiently "journey" (manipulate) the Quantum Flux Spectrum of Consciousness underlying one's present truth:

Here is a image of a windsurfer skimming effects along the sea's floor. While pretty professional, he's but very centered at the factors round him. The windsurfer is targeted upon how to show the sail. His question need to commonly be, "what am I going to do with the wind this is blowing proper now," instructs Kuan Yin.

There are the waves and the wind; visible and unseen forces. Everyone has those equal factors of their lives, the visible and unseen: karma and unfastened will. The query is, "How are you going to handle what you have got?" You're the usage of the karmic wave under and the wind can shift. Everyone have to take what they see and cope with that it in reality is unseen. Fall into the water!

Similar to the windsurfer inside the above parable, focus blissfully straddles the Quantum Flux Spectrum of Consciousness. Because of the Law of Consciousness Equilibrium, there is a constant, innate, propensity toward balancing the person's physical, intellectual, emotional and spiritual charge weather between Reality Framework One (Outer-Ego's visible, waking, linear truth) and Two (Inner-Ego's unseen, nonlinear truth). Through such moves, popularity will attempt to provide integration and amplification of the electricity ranges of recognition inside the Quantum Flux Spectrum of Consciousness essential for evolution/survival of the dreamer. Fall into the water is Kuan Yin's metaphor encouraging a person to help attain this balance thru way of delving into their unexplored intellectual territory of Framework Two's trance and desires.

Regard your All-That-Is due to the fact the Sun—the amplifier of all magnifications of consciousness; supply for all items and events manifested for your waking truth. Orbiting spherical one's Sun, then, is what might be imagined as one's Dream Planet. The next concentric circle might be everyday by using one's Trance Planet and similarly however, is one's Waking Planet. As one's Dream Planet orbits closest to its Sun, statistics it receives from this Source—this All-That-Is is probably more energizing—much less distorted then quantum records emanating from the Trance or Waking Planets.

Therefore, the farther every so-known as planet orbits from the Sun, the a great deal much less nonlinear its perceptual modality will become. And notwithstanding the truth that it could seem to the Outer Ego/Reasoning Mind that, in goals, its sequential-based totally commonplace experience/integrity has been have become upside-down, Inner Ego's quantum-primarily based commonplace experience/integrity is the right vibration-alignment with that of the Great Expansion of Consciousness: that agree with amongst those organizational Psychological Reality Frameworks is the catalyst for carrying out the last reason of successfully manipulating depend. Regain believe thru understanding: 1. Each second is a present day possibility, 2. Nothing is ever out of region and three. The vibration you offer to the universe will move again to you exactly in kind.

As Psychological Reality Framework Two/All-That-Is represents the countless shop of all recognized and unknown geographical regions, it offers an prolonged manner more numerous perceptions then can be imagined by way of way of the Outer Ego/Reasoning Mind. Performing separate but complimentary capabilities, Psychological Reality Framework One and Two procedures were intended to conform Outer-Ego's as an alternative slender perceptions. Yet, chronic distrust on the part of the Outer Ego/Reasoning Mind will drastically inhibit this technique. Distrust causing vibrational misalignment's among ego and the Inner Self is a primary cause for attracting undesirable, default realities.

Mistrust can come from a sense of loss/abandonment. When you fully recognize that each second is a present day possibility, no longer whatever is ever out of region and that the vibration you offer to the universe will go lower again to you exactly in type, you can regain your trust in existence.

Chapter 7: Your Relationship with Your Original Grace

Whatever the concern count of your dreams, their underlying reason is to inform you of your evolving relationship together with your Original Grace—that this is interested in you. Naturally, your waking-identification is ruled with the aid of using the usage of your values, modern interests and abilties. Indeed, whether or no longer one is a musical genius or has the capability to calm a bothered soul, every person has a expertise. The most important of these skills may be one's innate capability to create their maximum loved truth.

Misconceptions approximately demise are associated with misconceptions of what it's miles to be alive. Of this stuff you can be assured: popularity is the writer of each fact inside the multidimensional, vibrational Spectrum of Existence. As a reassurance to those overly-obsessed on the transport-loss of life cycle, endure in mind that each breath offers a extremely-present day possibility—a doorway to parallel existences often witnessed in desires; that we're, honestly, multidimensional beings having a secular lifestyles.

While one might also additionally come across, in goals, an enactment; a mimicking of a real lifestyles enjoy, the bulk of dreams provide a smorgasbord of identities and latent abilties to be had to the dreamer. And if the dreamer is absolutely too immutable in their strategies, they may enjoy dreams of being a little one—frequently a warning that they live too slender in their expectancies of themselves and have to increase their pastimes and definitions.

However, now not thinking of primary Law of Attraction thoughts bearing in mind the multidimensionality of one's thoughts gestalt, one may additionally moreover need to locate themselves absolutely reliant upon the usual pat symbolic definitions determined in dream dictionaries. Without using this Dream Analysis and Journaling for Your Best Life format through unraveling the ideals and their emotions inside the again of maximum any dream scenario, the right which means of 1's desires may additionally constantly elude them.

Confident that one's outer truth is a give up result of one's inner idea constructs, this type of method want to then lead the dreamer to healing the source of the transference of restricting idea constructs from one's Psychological Reality Framework Two to Psychological Reality Framework One. Utilizing the above procedure, it need to come to be apparent that goals were never an quit, but rather a technique through which the dreamer can open new avenues of expression that had previously been repressed; thereby resolving any hidden blockages to achievement.

Any overemphasis of a single identity can take location in desires as cool lively movie-like characters or situations. These varieties of goals can be regarded as awareness's gentle nudge encouraging the dreamer to open themselves to a greater expansive software program of their Original Grace—that they may be free to discover the happy opportunities existence has to offer. Investigating different capabilities and avenues for expression, one need to understand that because of the countless opportunities of the without delay, parallel realities can simultaneously be made out of latest identities and passions.

While abilities displayed in a unmarried's youth might also moreover additionally have been carried over from every other life, one's waking reality gives a outstanding opportunity to expand upon them. Meanwhile, there are fantastic, latent competencies watching for enough stimulus to rouse them. They lay just beyond the bounds of one's Outer-Ego/Reasoning Consciousness as deeply-held impulses that would, inside the blink of a watch, display themselves like stems bursting forth from fertile soil.

Dreaming of a former love dating summarized for me how even though a partnership in the end fizzles, it may however display useful in crystallizing someone's subsequent step in the adventure closer to Self-Fulfillment/Self-Love:

In the dream, my associate and I have been in short staying at every other couple's residence at the equal time as reputedly planning to relocate from our favored home-city. Noting his excessive exhilaration towards the flow into, I couldn't help however evaluation his pleasure with my as an opportunity sentimental, even reluctant, temper. Shortly thereafter, I found out that my preliminary hobby in him have become fast fading and that I was not inclined to excursion that existence path.

Indeed, thru carefully searching at his private strong imaginative and prescient of himself, I emerge as growing a clearer photo of the course I wanted to pursue in my lifestyles. I observed out that despite the fact that the connection had no longer worked out, my new revel in of self had awakened sound asleep talents—an in depth impetus to my cause as a creator.

Magical DNA! While some may persist in concerning it as actually a chemical (albeit vital to the shape and feature of all existence on earth), others would probable insist that it has its very personal interest—that its strange shape of attention allows for species edition and specialization. The concept that human reputation is magnetic, multidimensional and able to cross past time and location is supported by means of the usage of state-of-the-art quantum physics discoveries—that any 'beyond' fact is decided by using the usage of a 'future' thoughts confirmation of that truth.

Having remained dormant; reason-geared up to spring forth from the All-That-Is; a plethora of past and destiny devices and activities, one's internal impulses incorporate all the essential impetus for the blossoming of recent creativity inside the direction of every body issue in a unmarried's life. Perhaps one of the most essential revelations of embarking upon this method for dream evaluation is which you respect the first-rate complexity of your being.

I've said that the multidimensional communications/interactions straddling the Law of Attraction Probabilities/Frequencies Manifestation Gestalt—entities/intelligences modern even unimaginably prolonged distances apart have the potential to steer and alter one another. Earthly phenomena together with telepathy amongst nice gadgets of twins, a mom's intuition concerning her baby or the mom/fetus psychic connection all factor to Entanglement. Indeed, the universe we inhabit is not unintended. Everything is, in a few manner, related, purposeful and all of the possibilities exist already. In order to attract most effective one's most desired fact, replace any filters of fear or judgment with a greater splendid technique to life.

What are your passions? Even if you don't forget that mastering a present day venture is past your abilities, you despite the reality which have the potential to begin to expand formerly unexplored avenues of interest. Indeed, thru such exploration and development, you are creating parallel realities of opportunity and pleasure! How one strategies this form of aim, regardless of the reality that, is as important as making the selection to preserve. If, for instance, one affirms the pursuit can be handy and a laugh—and they'll get keep of any required help, they're installing a terrific vibration. If, but, one issues this form of pursuit may be not some factor however drudgery, they will experience a dream similar to the subsequent wherein the dreamer found herself at a party overflowing with human beings readying themselves for a few form of exercise. The dreamer persevered to offer an reason of:

Sensing the pride, I knew that most of the individuals inside the room were demanding to start. My interest piqued, I discovered myself following what others round me were doing. Facing the wall and shielding my head with my forearm, I waited for some thing to take area. Suddenly, someone threw a hardball up inside the air. Landing a few area else within the room, it fortuitously had now not hit every person. Another hardball then hurled, now not genuinely suddenly, thru the air. Now, I modified into becoming quite wary. Was this without a doubt a recreation I desired to pursue: taking the full-size chance that I or everyone else changed into going to be randomly hit with a hardball? Not enthralled with the possibilities of such volatile conduct, I hastily exited the room.

Trying to decipher the metaphorical which means of my dream, I determined out we each have a choice to play the sport of duck and cowl or increase the skills of being constructive about evolving one's abilities. Such optimism will then trap lifestyles conditions bolstering one's real cause to beautify their lifestyles.

Head injuries can be exceedingly debilitating or maybe reason loss of life. Yet, the people in my dream persevered to hazard everything for the sake of this hobby of mysterious outcomes. It is especially tough to assess what is coming your manner even as your head hangs low and is covered thru your forearm. After a while, no longer most effective do you agree with you haven't any manipulate over the severa random gadgets flying thru the air, you can thoroughly begin to don't forget top notch, even more threats. Another interpretation of the dream is that thoughts are topics and that once we ship out horrible thoughts, they could come lower lower again as terrible idea paperwork sapping our strength or (after gaining mass) as materialized items and events.

In what appeared like a look at-up dream, I noticed myself leaving a celebration. Rushing upstairs to my condo, I located on the middle of the room what seemed to be an normal parking meter. Venturing nearer, however, I found out that one of the coin slots modified into marked penance, the opportunity, opportunity:

On earth, you can typically choose, a voice from beyond shouted. As if to expose me the manner, some airy hand located 1 / 4 within the opportunity slot.

Worry and specific inhibiting idea projections are maximum genuinely no longer the cause of creativeness. With those super minds of ours, we're meant to expect the maximum expansive opportunities. Some lesser truth can be seemed as an accumulation of incomplete or misguided idea paperwork. It is because of the truth the earth offers us diverse and infinite possibilities to definitely discover, indeed take a look at the waters, it's miles this gift; this realistic life offering an possibility for self-awareness. The following dream explains the splendid expansiveness of Psychological Reality Framework Two; how it could release you from the monotony and fear whilst adhering to best your Outer-Ego definitions and identification:

Venturing out into the darkness, I positioned myself at the brink of a small harbor. Drawn via the plaintive calls of the moored boats, I watched as some historical wind taunted the lashed sails. One craft in particular seized my interest. Completely entranced, I found out it bore a remarkable resemblance to an oil portray I'd deserted at the shore. Gingerly, I stepped onto a single wood plank, the simplest apparent path to the boat. Edging earlier, I couldn't realize whether or not this slim beam have turn out to be an actual dock or without a doubt flotsam at the water. Nearing its surrender, my body weight unexpectedly crushed the flimsy and treacherous board, submerging it, and me collectively with it.

Then, I felt my body bypass deep below the waves; what may in the long run be my personal sounding of the depths of focus. Gasping, I in the end shot out of the big and mysterious waters, again into waking truth.

It is in the limitless, timeless ocean of Psychological Reality Framework Two; that these layered realities, like waves, will shape and reform: building into towering monuments or surely washing away. Maintain religion that during spite of apparent human frailties and foibles, we're a resilient species and there are limitless possibilities within a quantum universe to take region our most goals.

Chapter 8: Lucid Dreams

While in big element shunning the concept of awakening internal its exchange bandwidths of trance and dreams, Outer-Ego has an ongoing interest of its Greater Self and that, at any time, it may satisfy its birthright; forging new innovative parameters. It is this intention; this high-quality prize that souls incarnating on this earth are searching out.

While Outer-Ego is usually laser-centered in the beta (waking) pulse, due to the species participation in the Great Expansion of Consciousness, there are various stages of shared facts flexibility amongst Framework One and Two. For instance, there are those who can be greater mentally-acclimated to the alpha (trance) pulse; often slipping from beta to an alpha semi-trance state all through their each day routine. Having advanced to skillfully straddle their absolutely-alert beta nation with their alpha nation, the ones humans have advanced this proclivity; maximizing advantages inside this exchange thoughts u.S.. Similarly, folks that more resultseasily navigate their dreams exemplify humanity's genuine origins because of the truth the Dream Alchemists.

Are you a greater Outward or Inward Person? Do you supply more validity to your waking international or in your goals? Even in case you don't forget yourself a staunchly Outward Person, in this period of technological wonders wherein the thoughts can get exhausted via the use of the usage of the maze of linear stimuli, it's reassuring to understand that everybody has the functionality to advantage intensely-interactive, nonlinear Lucid Dreaming.

In goals, sequential interactions now not take a look at because of the fact the enjoy of beyond and destiny vanishes inner this nonlinear medium of Framework Two. Whereas non-lucid goals are typically skilled as dim or burdened replicas of 1's waking reality, the characters, vicinity, sounds, bodily and emotional emotions, and so forth., professional in Lucid Dreams are typically more vividly-skilled then those in 3-D waking reality. Thus, in Lucid Dreams, one well-knownshows themselves aware in their extremely-centered dream surroundings wherein gadgets and sports can, with practice, be manipulated with the aid of the use of a trifling notion. Additionally, in preference to the same vintage perceived behind schedule actualization in waking truth, thoughts and emotions exhibited in Lucid Dreams can bring about immediately manifestation, thereby showing the actual nature of advent.

Similar to the producing of a movement picture in which an assemblage of casting, script, sound, lighting, get dressed, make-up and technical, and so forth. Experts is wanted, the producing of a Lucid Dream calls for the complete hobby of its producer—you! You may no longer, for instance, bring together as a backdrop for a modern comedy, some grim, medieval degree set. Nor, may additionally you solid actors having no familiarity with the nuances in their person or of getting not have a observe the script. Everything, from the man or woman's dialect to makeup to facial expressions, should be proper!

As producer as well as all the characters and scenery within the intimate space of your desires, you're mastering to skillfully instill your dream manufacturing with talents that in form your particular dreams and tastes. There are mind internal thoughts, geographical areas inside nation-states. Because of the Law of Attraction, you continuously draw out of your dream worldwide the ones realities maximum intently mirroring your number one ideals and values. Therefore, stay aware of your mind and emotions similarly to gadgets and sports provided for your Lucid Dream, for his or her next keep you could be your waking truth!

In my private Lucid Dream, I couldn't assist however agree with it changed into showing me belonging to three superior parallel species at the identical time as concurrently being human:

Awakening from what had appeared like a legitimate sleep, the whole lot appeared so actual! Initially believing I modified into however myself in my very own female frame, seconds later I discovered out I changed into in some manner every a woman and man; an androgynous being having quick jet black hair and translucent, even glowing pores and skin. Dressed in black, leotard-like garb, my eyes had been incredible crystal blue. Realizing I became dwelling aboard a spaceship, I marveled on the very modern décor and technology.

Approaching the noticeably-superior scientific middle on board, this parallel me; this androgynous self, modified into scheduled for a few type of eye surgical operation. All the while, this being had an attention of my woman counterpart living on the planet. Coincidentally, this grow to be a period in my earth lifestyles once I changed into scheduled to have a cancerous increase removed from above my right eye.

While having a awesome fondness for my earthly counterpart, this 'superior' model of me seemingly appeared my human shape as actually primitive. Preparing my androgynous self psychologically for surgical procedure, I had entire faith in those very geared up docs. I heard one of the spaceship scientific docs say, This surgical treatment may even help the parallel you this is residing in the global alongside side her eye trouble. Awakening naked from that dream, I determined the nightgown I'd previously donned, folded well; teetering at the out of doors of the bed. Indeed, I had no memory of ever removing my nightgown. Nor would possibly I simply have folded it and placed it inside the form of precarious function.

When, in a while, my waking-truth surgical remedy transpired with none headaches, I wondered if the calming terms, intentions and moves taking location in that outer-area realm had a few element to do with the excessive great final results proper proper right here inside the global. That my androgynous self believed my female counterpart inside the international to be a fairly primitive appeared to confirm a broadly-everyday idea in metaphysical circles—that most effective in quite evolutionarily-primitive civilizations is there sexual dimorphism. It is likewise clean from the dream that I concurrently understood the mindsets and bodily nature of every the outer-area model and earthly me.

In but each one-of-a-kind UFO Lucid Dream, I unexpectedly woke up into what appeared to be over again and vicinity. Sensing my husband, John, inside the room, I could not arouse him. Gazing from the window on the starry sky, there traveled a darkish disk in the course of the face of the moon. Dashing into the night time time time; looking at the heavens, nary a touch of the vessel may additionally moreover want to now be seen! Longing for its go back, I solemnly walked returned to the residing.

Then, dreaming of sitting under a radio tower hovering immoderate into the clouds; sensing the various frequencies, I even have end up aware that the radio wave transmissions were extensions of my very very own interest! The message therein changed into the subsequent: The Quantum Flux Spectrum is much like a band of radio channels encompassing each the restricting vibration anger and worry channels to the expansive vibration loving-kindness channels. Which channel do you want amplified and integrated into your life? Lifting the 'veil' of Psychological Reality Framework One; deliberating a greater experience of oneself, you may be capable of awaken to awareness's limitless, expansive principles of itself.

Around that same time, I dreamt the following: sticky from the residue of some protracted sleep, my 1/3 eye felt as though it were tightly close for a totally long term. Feeling it slowly open, I knew this event may also allow for extended conscious processing of information in the change, nonlinear geographical areas; those vibration levels beyond waking attention defensive data generally unavailable to the waking thoughts. Drifting into every other 1/2 of-sleep; surprised at my complete-radius functionality to apprehend some distance past my instantaneous environment, my 1/3 eye became now surely open. Emerging from my forehead-aspect, a wiry stalk with blooming lotus at its tip, curled round and round, accomplishing into infinity.

Another Lucid Dream confirmed, resting from her day in the maximum inhospitable of glens and crags, the Welsh mom goddess, Danu cradling a wee fairy babe within the palm of her hand. Nearby, like no earthen flora, changed into the Mythical Tree; dew-kissed, crimson and white bellflowers bowing its weighted down branches. My eyes straying from this sincere sight for however a right away, I located out, with wonderful wonder, that as the kid grew, so too might also the tree's thoughts-blowing blooms! Heaving in the wind, the tree; with thick roots clutched deep into the difficult-hewn rock, then stood steady. One via one, its blossoms drifted at some stage in the steep, craggy cliffs; right all the manner all the way down to the paranormal waters, wherein crimson lotus blossoms bobbed upon the whitecaps as a long manner as the attention need to see!

Now, we youngsters by manner of hook or through criminal knew that everywhere the plant life scattered, there could be fantastic caches of gold.

Dare I make that daunting soar? I pondered, even as searching the red petals glide farther and farther at the wind. It was then I noticed the older boys, reputedly with out a care, dive off the cliff; disappearing into the azure waves and then bobbing to the floor.

Lured through the promise of riches—of the unknown, I amassed all courage I knew to be mine. Curiosity peaked, I stood poised on that terrific precipice. Fearing my bones would possibly honestly shatter upon effect, I however the fact that took a deep breath and leapt into the waters that lay a protracted way under. My body slamming the waves, it drifted down into the darkish, bloodless depths of the sea. Gasping for air, I ultimately surfaced; swimming appropriately to shore.

Chapter 9: Dream interpretation in numbers

Dream interpretation in numbers is an historical exercising that goals to decode the which means that of goals the usage of mathematical symbols.

For instance, the number one would possibly represent introduction, on the identical time as the amount nine need to constitute completeness. Using this method, some dreamers receive as authentic with they may advantage belief into their subconscious mind and higher recognize their waking life. While there can be no clinical proof to guide this claim, some people find out comfort and guidance in dream interpretation with the aid of the usage of numbers. If you're dreaming of effective numbers, here are some interpretations to get you started:

-1: The #1 often symbolizes advent or starting.

-2: The quantity 2 regularly symbolizes balance, duality, or cooperation.

-The quantity 3 often symbolizes increase or creativity.

-The big range four frequently symbolizes balance or basis.

-The range 5 often symbolizes exchange or development.

(6) The range 6 regularly symbolizes love, compassion, and restoration.

7) The range 7 often symbolizes know-how or religious popularity.

-The variety eight regularly symbolizes power or abundance.

-The variety nine often symbolizes completeness or endings.

Dreams are a way for our brains to approach facts and kind through reminiscences. Dreams can be interpreted in numbers to provide us insights into our lives. By paying attention to the range sequences that seem in our goals, we will advantage treasured perception into what's taking region in our lives on a subconscious degree. If you would like assist decoding your dream collection, please attain out to us for assist.

Dream interpretation in Zulu

Dream interpretation in Zulu is considered to be a sacred hobby. The desires of an individual are seen as messages from the ancestors, and it's miles crucial to interpret them efficaciously if you want to recognize the choice of the spirits. Dreams can be interpreted to assume the destiny, supply steerage on vital alternatives, or warn of risk. There are many symbols and pictures that can appear in dreams, and every has its very own meaning. To interpret a dream, one want to first understand the context in which it befell and the emotions that have been felt in it.

Dream interpretation isn't always simplest used to understand the choice of the ancestors but also to diagnose problems with the living. If there may be a war in a person's existence, or if they may be tormented by an contamination, it could appear itself in their desires. The goals of a pregnant girl also can be interpreted to decide the health of her unborn toddler. In Zulu way of life, goals are taken into consideration very powerful and ought to not be taken gently.

One of the most well-known dream interpreters in Zulu records modified into Credo Mutwa. He is stated to have had the potential to interpret the dreams of animals in addition to human beings. He used his information of wants to help humans apprehend the preference of the ancestors and diagnose problems with the residing.

Dreams are a way for human beings to approach the sports in their day and paintings thru problems. Dreams additionally may be a supply of facts or steering. The interpretation of goals is an critical a part of Zulu way of lifestyles. In order to apprehend anyone's dream, it is critical to comprehend the man or woman's background and existence tale. This permits to provide context to the symbols in the dream. By information desires, Zulu human beings can gain perception into their non-public lives and the lives of others.

Islam interprets desires.

Islam translates dreams as a manner of speaking with Allah. Dreams may be interpreted in many tactics and often consist of hidden messages for the dreamer. Muslims are advocated to write down down down their dreams and to are looking for interpretation from an authorized Islamic pupil inside the occasion that they have any questions or issues approximately their goals. Some of the maximum commonplace dream symbols embody end give up end result, animals, water, houses, and people. Dreams can be interpreted to symbolize non secular states, caution messages, or glimpses into the destiny.

Islamic subculture teaches us that dreams are a manner for Allah to talk alongside together with his lovers. Dreams can frequently include hidden messages or warnings for the dreamer. Muslims are encouraged to put in writing down their goals and to looking for interpretation from an authorized Islamic student inside the occasion that they have got any questions or problems about their desires. Some of the maximum commonplace dream symbols encompass cease end result, animals, water, homes, and those. Dreams may be interpreted to symbolize spiritual states, caution messages, or glimpses into the destiny.

Type of dream in Islam

There are 3 most vital varieties of dreams in Islam:

1. Ru'ya—this is the most not unusual form of dream, and it is truly a glimpse into the spiritual worldwide.

2. Hulm—that may be a dream this is because of ingesting effective food, ingesting alcohol, or smoking cigarettes.

three. Maree—that may be a dream that is because of magic or witchcraft.

The non secular meaning of goals in Islam

Many Muslims take delivery of as true with that desires may be interpreted to offer glimpses into the future or to expose spiritual truths. Dreams may also be interpreted as messages from Allah or as warnings for the dreamer. It is considered crucial to pay close to attention to at least one's dreams and to are searching for guidance from an authorized Islamic student if there are any questions or troubles about a particular dream.

Biblical dream interpretation:

The interpretation of biblical dreams is a fascinating issue count number that has been studied with the aid of humans sooner or later of statistics. There are many first rate interpretations of biblical desires, and it is able to be hard to decide what they endorse. However, with some information and information of biblical symbolism, it's far often feasible to interpret biblical dreams.

One of the most famous examples of biblical dream interpretation is the story of Joseph within the Bible. Joseph modified into capable of interpret Pharaoh's dream and its which means that. This helped him turn out to be one of the maximum effective guys in Egypt.

There are many wonderful techniques that can be used for biblical dream interpretation. One crucial detail to do not forget is that biblical desires typically have a deeper that means than truly what's taking place at the floor. It is often essential to have a have a look at the larger image which will apprehend a biblical dream.

Biblical desires may be interpreted in lots of one-of-a-kind methods, and there may be no one right interpretation for each dream. However, with some understanding of biblical symbolism and interpretation strategies, it is regularly possible to loose up the which means of biblical goals.

Unlocking the which means that of biblical desires

It can be a fascinating and worthwhile revel in. It can help us to recognize the Bible better and to see the world in a one-of-a-type mild. Dreams are regularly a manner for God to speak with us, and biblical dream interpretation may be a effective tool for statistics His message.

When decoding biblical desires, it's far vital to keep an open mind and now not try to force any precise interpretation. There isn't always each person right solution for each dream. Instead, it's far critical to allow the biblical symbolism to guide us as we try to free up the this means that of the dream. With practice, biblical dream interpretation can grow to be less difficult and additional correct.

The Bible is full of testimonies about people who had prophetic goals, and those goals often contained messages from God. Biblical dream interpretation may be a powerful manner to get in the course of Him and to understand His will for our lives. By understanding the this means that of biblical desires, we will learn how to higher interpret the messages that God is attempting to deliver us.

Dreams interpretation within the Bible is a precious device to know-how our subconscious mind. What we dream about can provide insights into our thoughts, feelings and dreams that we may be ignorant of during our waking hours. While now not all goals have an obvious which means that, analyzing them can assist us benefit greater self-reputation or even prophetic perception. If you're interested in exploring the arena of desires interpretation, the Bible is a splendid place to begin. Have you ever interpreted considered one of your private desires? What modified into the enjoy like for you?

Dreams interpretation

One of the maximum thrilling and mysterious factors of the human enjoy is desires. Dreams are enigmatic and charming, and their which means that is frequently difficult to interpret. Though goals had been interpreted in masses of diverse strategies over the years, there are some desired meanings which might be commonly normal.

Some dream professionals be given as real with that dreams are a way for the subconscious thoughts to speak with the aware thoughts. Dreams can be a way for your unconscious to speak hidden dreams or fears, or to provide you guidance on the manner to resolve a problem. Other professionals believe that desires are a way in your mind to approach records from your day by day existence. This can include some element from sports that befell during the day to stuff you noticed or heard.

There isn't always any right or incorrect interpretation of dreams; it's far as an awful lot as you to determine what your desires mean to you. However, in case you are interested by dream interpretation, there are a few subjects to hold in thoughts. First, desires may be symbolic and frequently have a couple of meanings. When decoding your dreams, it is essential to be aware of the statistics of your desires similarly to your emotions and emotions. Additionally, it's miles useful to preserve a dream mag so that you can song your dreams through the years and see if any patterns emerge. If you are nevertheless unsure about the that means of a dream, it could be useful to are trying to find recommendation from an expert. Dreams provide us a very specific perception into our unconscious minds and can offer valuable steerage on the manner to clear up troubles or issues in our lives.

Abandon

To dream that you are abandoned method that you can. You can also have trouble framing your plans for future fulfillment.

Abandonment may be a completely frightening enjoy. It can leave you feeling isolated and by myself. When you dream of being abandoned, it is also a sign that you're feeling some worry or lack of self belief in your waking life. You also can enjoy like you're all by myself inside the global and that no man or woman is acquainted with or cares approximately you.

There may be many motives for why you sense deserted. It may be that you have these days lengthy gone via a annoying experience, collectively with a divorce or the death of a cherished one. You may also additionally furthermore experience deserted if you are going through a tough time for your lifestyles, together with unemployment or infection.

If you feel deserted, it is crucial to attain out for useful useful resource. There are many individuals who care about you and need to assist. Talk to your pals and own family humans, or are searching for expert assist if you need it. The most important problem is to now not isolate yourself from the folks who love you. You can not overcome abandonment to your non-public - permit others in and they'll help you heal.

Accident.

To dream of being in an coincidence denotes that you may have unfortunate revel in on your company or amorous affairs.

However, it is critical to bear in mind that goals are not generally prophetic. Sometimes they will be in truth manifestations of our fears or anxieties. If you're especially worried approximately a few aspect, it's far likely that you'll dream approximately it. So, do no longer panic when you have a dream about being in an twist of fate. It might now not typically advise that a few thing horrible goes to stand up. The super manner to address such desires is to try to figure out what they might be representing on your waking existence. Are there any regions of your lifestyles in that you revel in like you are headed for a crash? If so, then maybe the dream is a caution from your unconscious to take things more slowly. On the alternative hand, in case you're usually happy with the way your existence is going, then the dream may be a signal that you're in over your head. In either case, it's miles an brilliant concept to take a better take a look at the scenario and note if there are any adjustments you need to make. Accidents may be very steeply-priced each financially and emotionally, so it's high-quality to avoid them if the least bit feasible.

Actor

To dream of seeing an actor on the degree denotes the satisfied consummation of doubtful affairs. If you're an actor, you may be successful in making new buddies.

Actor goals can also suggest that you are organized to move on from a tough situation. Seeing an actor on your dream also can represent a hidden issue of yourself that you are geared up to carry out into the open. Alternatively, the dream may be prompting you to perform that and stay greater authentically. If you aren't happy together collectively along with your modern-day profession, then this dream also can moreover advocate which you must hold in mind turning into an actor. Acting is all about pretending to be someone else, which can be interpreted as symbolizing your want to precise your self in a way that is wonderful out of your ordinary person. On a greater awful word, actor dreams may additionally moreover constitute your worry of being exposed or inclined. If you are uncomfortable with a few element of your life, the dream can be prompting you to accomplish that and deal with the ones troubles.

Addition

To dream of addition way that you'll have an increase for your family or industrial business corporation. This may be within the shape of extra cash, extra assets, or extra individuals of your organization. Whatever the boom is, it will bring you delight and pleasure. A dream of addition also may be a sign that you are prepared to move immediately to the following chapter in your lifestyles. Be open to new opportunities that come your way!

So, what do you believe you studied? Additional dreams can be a actually fine signal, indicating that right subjects are coming your way. Be open to new possibilities and phrase how the subsequent monetary disaster in your existence unfolds!

Adam and Eve have been made.

To dream about Adam and Eve manner which you could no longer have a danger to achieve success for your business commercial enterprise employer.

Betrayal and terrible religion will make your fortune crumble if you see them collectively in the garden. Adam is sporting a fig leaf, however Eve is sincerely naked except for an oriental-colored snake on her waist and stomach.

It foretells that clever girls will lose their reputation and recognition due to the fact they communicate to the serpent.

The snake is a image of temptation, and the dream indicates that you may succumb to it if you are not cautious. The snake on Eve's frame will also be interpreted as a sexual dream.

Seeing them run across the Garden of Eden way that some fantastic occasion is set to show up. The addition for your dream can also additionally propose that you are searching out a child. This dream is normally considered to be an amazing omen.

Adderall XR

One of your buddies, who's lifeless but although appears to be mendacity at the floor and respiration, partly rises to a sitting function at the equal time as the viper hits him, and then each of them disappear into close by wood. This technique that you will be very sad for each of them and your self.

This way that a person who is not telling the reality may be the only to motive her problems. If he runs a ways from her, she may be capable of shield her individual whilst people say awful subjects about it.

Admire

To dream which you are widely known way that you may keep the love of your antique friends, in spite of the reality that your new characteristic will located you above them. Admiring a person to your dream way which you are looking as a top notch deal as that character and might even want to be like them. This is an indication of proper subjects to return back for you. Seeing a person you dislike being nicely-liked in your dream approach that the scenario or trouble you are coping with will speedy be resolved. Admire can also be interpreted as a caution now not to permit your ego get too huge. Stay humble and live authentic to your self, and others will recognize you for it.

Adopted

Seeing your followed little one or determine for your desires manner that you may convey excellent success through the schemes and speculations of humans you do not understand.

If you dream that you or others are adopting a little one, you could make an unlucky alternate for your dwelling house.

Adultery

In your goals, it method that you'll be punished for committing a criminal offense. If a woman has this dream, it's miles going to be tough for her to hold her husband's hobby. Her character and wickedness will crush them at any possibility. If her buddy's husband is along side her husband, his husband will no longer be aware about her. If he does this, his rights may be cruelly violated. So in this situation, if she thinks she is encouraging a greater younger man or woman to try this, she ought to break up.

For a young female, this indicates debasement and low dreams, wherein case she will be able to discover bizarre adventures appealing.

It is mostly a remarkable concept to dream that you had been capable of fight off any temptation. Giving in is wrong. There are vampiric influences that surround a person who has low morals. They are organized to help him collectively along with his evil plans.

These sorts of dreams can handiest be due to wicked factors. If someone chooses lofty ideals, he may be enlightened by the divine precept interior him and may be free from lustful dreams. The guy who denies the lifestyles and electricity of evil spirits has no arcane or occult expertise. Is Simon Magus, the sorcerer, a healthy for the black magicians of Pharaoh's time or the guys of God? The sweetheart dreamer who's in love is usually recommended to be cautious no longer to get caught.

Adulation

If you dream that you need people to like you, it approach that you could placed on a display to get honors you do no longer deserve.

If you reward someone, you could give up a cherished club within the preference that it will assist your material dreams.

Advancement

To dream of shifting ahead in any engagement suggests your fast ascent closer to marketing and marketing choice.

People who circulate in advance are awaiting that your buddies will be in appropriate locations near you.

If you conquer an opponent, you'll escape the outcomes of a intense disaster.

Adventurer

When you dream that you're the sufferer of an adventurer, because of this you'll be clean prey for flatterers and villains inside the real global. You could have a tough time getting your subjects to be the identical consistency.

She may be too targeted on her very private moves to look that she is being complimented, this means that that that she can be able to not be able to see that she is grateful.

Adversity

A lousy dream technique that you may fail and function horrible topics seem time and again yet again.

For a person who has a whole lot of hysteria approximately how matters paintings, seeing different people in a lousy state of affairs may be a lousy sign.

Old dream books say that could be a sign of suitable matters to return. This definition is incorrect.

In a person, there are forces at artwork. One comes from internal and the opposite comes from outside. They come from one-of-a-kind worlds: the animal spirit, it's far stimulated with the useful resource of the personal international of carnal preference, and the spiritual spirit of the kingdom of time-commemorated brotherhood, which has an opposing motif in the dreamer's mind. They every come from terrific worlds. If the ones forces labored collectively, or if the dreamer's thoughts changed into whole of a photograph of a actual-existence success, great frame sensations ought to make the dreamer revel in horrible interior. Having some of coins to your frame makes the mind's have an impact on for your soul a lot much less powerful than it must be. It's commonplace for the spirit to be happy and the body to be sad at the same time as topics pass wrong. People who are worldly dreamers also can moreover see development in the event that they listen the cry of a saddened spirit of their desires. This isn't the concept of occult forces that made this e-book what it's miles.

Adultery

A dream of adultery foretells that you will be unfortunate on your engagements and love affairs. You may additionally lose cash and assets via speculation.

If you are experiencing a dream approximately adultery, it could be interpreted as a caution from your unconscious thoughts. This dream is regularly visible as a signal that you will be unfortunate in your present day amorous affairs. You may additionally lose coins or belongings due to some type of hypothesis.

aeroplane

A dream of being on an airplane denotes a trade for the higher for your affairs.

Dreaming of an plane also can advise a choice for extra freedom or a want for exchange. It may moreover represent a trendy starting or a modern-day phase in your life. If you're afraid to fly, this dream can also additionally mirror your worry of change. Alternatively, it is able to endorse that you aren't prepared for the changes which can be beforehand. Whatever the because of this that, this dream is clearly certainly certainly really worth exploring further.

Affairs

To dream of your private affairs being made public manner that you can have problem for your business organization existence and social individuals of the own family. If you dream that others are speakme about your affairs, it foretells that you will be the task of adverse gossip.

A dream that you are afraid manner that you could have a worried breakdown or an emotional disturbance. It might also additionally represent a few worry or tension which you are currently experiencing to your waking lifestyles. This dream may be attempting to tell you which you need to be privy to your emotional well-being. If you're continuously feeling anxious or forced out, it can take a toll to your intellectual fitness. Make nice to take some time for your self and lighten up. Maybe perform a little yoga or meditation to help you chill out. Alternatively, if there may be something particular that is making you scared or annoying, attempt to face it head-on. Don't let your fears control your existence!

Afterlife

To dream of the afterlife approach that exquisite modifications will take region to your right now future in case you want to result in each suitable or lousy fortune. It may additionally moreover moreover constitute a few detail of yourself this is currently vain or dormant.

agent

To dream of an insurance agent manner that you'll be unfortunate in love and business enterprise affairs. To see an insurance agent to your dream means that a few terrible event is prepared to reveal up. You can be feeling inclined and unprotected. Alternatively, the coverage agent may additionally constitute part of yourself that is careful and conservative. Consider what attributes of the coverage agent are pondered in your personal personality. To dream that you are an coverage agent shows which you need to take greater care at the side of your personal affairs. You can be too careless or optimistic in your movements. Alternatively, this dream symbolizes your feelings of being blanketed and cared for.

Alcohol

To dream which you are consuming alcohol shows which you are searching out some form of break out or consolation from your problems. The dream may also be a caution in the direction of immoderate drinking. The key factor to recollect is that alcohol can be very volatile, every physically and mentally, so it is essential to drink sparsely in case you do choose to drink

Getting Old

A dream about ageing is terrible records for any form of commercial business enterprise.

To dream approximately your age way that your household might be angry at you because of how you watched.

She'll be in lousy company and her denial of what humans say can be taken as a humorous tale. Seeing oneself as antique foreshadows a likely or ugly contamination. There is a chance of her dropping her lover if he grows antique at the identical time as she sees him.

Agony

It isn't as beautiful as some people assume. There may be some fear and combined feelings, however greater of the number one than of the second one.

Agony over the lack of cash or assets method that you have disturbing and imaginary fears about the important nation of things or the health of near friends or family.

See them cry.

Air

This dream approach that the dreamer goes to have a horrible time.

You may be introduced approximately do terrible subjects because of the reality you'll be forced into it.

Feeling cold air method that there are gaps for your commercial enterprise corporation and topics that do not work together.

A curse will fall on you in case you revel in oppressed with the aid of the usage of manner of the humidity. This curse will make your high-quality visions of the destiny offer way and close to on top of them.

Alabaster

To dream of alabaster way that you could have a excellent marriage and do properly in different crucial matters. Breaking an alabaster parent or vase shows that you are sorry and want to change. This way that the younger lady will lose her lover or his cash because of the fact she did not be privy to his recognition.

Alarm clock earrings.

When you concentrate a bell for your sleep, it method that you need to be afraid.

Album

An album approach that you'll be a success and make real friends if you dream about having one for your desires.

Seeing photographs in an album in your desires method that you may brief find a new lover who is going to be happy with you. This is a wonderful signal.

Alley

If you dream approximately an alleyway, it manner that your success will not be as proper because it became. There might be masses of factors that trouble you.

For a younger lady to stroll down an alley at night time time, it tells him that friendships have a awful reputation and that he himself has a horrible reputation.

Alloy

In your business, there can be masses of things an wonderful way to make you indignant. For a woman to dream of an alloy, there is a lot of pain, and the pain covers up the pleasure. Alloy is a mixture of or extra metals, and it's far regularly used to make a few element stronger. When you're alloyed with ache, it could be difficult to appearance the delight on your existence. But do not surrender in your dreams- keep preventing for what makes you satisfied. There is continuously mild at the cease of the tunnel.

Alum

The alum visible in a dream portends the frustration of properly-installed plans. It represents regret for considered one of your movements towards an innocent person, in keeping with the flavor of alum.

For a woman, dreaming about an entire lot of alum way that she could be dissatisfied in her marriage and lose her love.

Aluminum

To dream of aluminum way that you're happy along side your cash, no matter how small it's far. For a girl to appearance her aluminum adorns or rusty dishes way she can be sad and lose subjects that she didn't expect to lose.

Amateur

To dream of seeing an newbie actor on stage means that you can see your hopes fulfilled pleasantly and satisfactorily. In a tragedy, the lousy will spread thru your happiness. If there are blurry or distorted pictures in the dream, you're probable to stumble upon a quick and decisive defeat in a few organisation apart from your ordinary commercial enterprise enterprise.

Ambush

To dream which you are being attacked via an ambush method that you are hiding near some trouble an fantastic manner to return down and knock you down in case you are not careful.

If you are planning to get all over again at someone, you won't hesitate to do subjects that are not very brilliant for your friends.

America

Senior officers have to be careful for nation affairs; others will do properly to attend to their personal human beings, due to the fact problem is handy after this dream.

Dreaming of America is more than just a patriotic perfect. It's a manner of existence, a attitude that prioritizes opportunity and achievement. For generations, human beings have come to America in search of a higher lifestyles. And for hundreds, that dream has become a fact.

America is the land of possibility. Anyone can acquire something they set their mind to, regardless of what their statistics may be. That's what makes America so unique. It's an area in which each person may be a success, no matter their race or ethnicity.

The American Dream is alive and well. And it is more available than ever in advance than. All you want is the choice to achieve it and the strength of mind to make it display up. So do now not allow all and sundry permit you to recognise that the American Dream is lifeless. It's alive and properly, and it's miles ready so you can gain it.

Amethyst

People who see amethyst in a dream are happy after they do business enterprise corporation in a sincere way.

For a younger woman, losing an amethyst predicts that she may be in a position to interrupt up with her companion and feature romantic issues.

Ammonia

An ammonia dream manner that when the dreamer drives a friend, she or he may be unhappy. This dream results in fights and breakups of friendships.

It will be very probable that a greater younger female may be deceived via the person and intentions of a person she thinks is nice.

Ammunition

To dream of ammunition foretells the begin of a task that allows you to attain success. If you dream that your ammunition has run out, it technique that you may no longer be able to combat or strive.

Chapter 10: When you're in love, you do not

It's a awful concept to dream approximately being in love due to the reality your personal desires and pleasures are interior of you.

For a more youthful lady, this portends an illicit engagement, until she chooses in a stilted and moral manner a companion. For a married lady, it way she might be sad and need to have fun out of doors the residence.

Seeing different fanatics predicts that you may be persuaded to overlook your morals. People who see animals this manner are probably to have sex with short men or women.

Amputation

Ordinary amputation of limbs technique that someone has out of region a small method; if a person loses each legs or every hands, it way that the exchange is down. For sailors, storms and the lack in their subjects display up. The individual who had this dream need to be cautioned to be careful.

Almanac

An almanac dream method wonderful fortunes and faux pleasures. Reading the signs, you may determine out what's going to rise up. You'll be anxious via little subjects a good way to take some time.

Almonds

This is proper records. He has a number of coins. However, grief accompanies it for a quick on the identical time as. If the almonds are defective, your unhappiness in getting a positive want might be whole until new situations are created.

Alms

Almsgiving is awful, no matter the truth that it's miles given or interested by pride. Otherwise, a first rate dream.

Alms House

For a younger woman to dream of an alms residence approach that she will be capable of come upon a failure in her try to enter into a worldly marriage.

Altar

A dream about a priest at the altar foretells of squabbles and unsatisfactory conditions to your business business enterprise and domestic.See a marriage from grief to buddies, loss of life to vintage age.

You would possibly now not be established an altar in a dream and agree to tell humans not to carry out a bit thing wrong. The word "repentance" is likewise used.

Alligator

To dream of an alligator shows hidden enemies and dangerous passions.

Amber

Dreaming of amber foretells plenty correct fortune and plenty of blessings will come to you.

Dreaming of this translucent golden mineral is frequently associated with receiving a signal from the universe that all can be nicely. It is likewise visible as a harbinger of fabric wealth and exceptional properly fortune in corporation ventures. If you are lucky enough to discover a piece of amber, maintain it near you as it's far stated to preserve its proprietor happiness, health and suitable luck.

Ambulance

A dream of seeing or using in an ambulance on your dream denotes surprising infection or lack of existence on your circle of relatives. For a younger woman to look an ambulance warns her of illicit love, with a purpose to result in heartache.

America

To dream of America shows massive prosperity and success.

Anchor

The anchor in your desires foretells that you may be stored from a horrible business corporation deal by the use of the firmness of your cause. It is also a signal of stability and protection.

Androgyny

To dream which you are androgynous indicates that you are having hassle locating your identification or characteristic in lifestyles. You may be feeling overwhelmed or out of place inside the propose time.

Angel

Seeing an angel to your desires suggests divine steerage and safety. You are experiencing a time of non secular growth and awakening.

Animal cover

A dream of animal cover suggests that you are attempting to protect yourself from a few emotional hurt or trauma. You can be feeling vulnerable and uncovered inside the advise time.

Ankle

A dream of your ankle denotes a few instability on your affairs. If you injure your ankle inside the dream, it's miles a warning to be able to take extra care in the way you behavior yourself in company dealings or you'll undergo losses.

Anna Karenina

To dream of Anna Karenina shows unhappy unions and sickly offspring.

Anniversary

To dream of an anniversary foretells a happy occasion a first-rate way to supply plenty delight to you and your family.

An anonymous letter

Receiving an nameless letter to your goals foretells that you'll be the recipient of some unwelcome news.

Ants

Ants in goals usually represent tough artwork and industry. They also can furthermore represent a worry of invasion or being beaten.

apple

A dream of apples suggests top fulfillment, fertility, and health. Seeing a inexperienced apple for your dream symbolizes

possibility, growth, and new beginnings. Seeing a red apple in your dream symbolizes temptation and ardour. Eating an apple for your dream shows fitness and physical nicely-being. Coring an apple for your dream shows which you are exploring your sexuality. To dream that you are bitten by using the usage of an apple shows that you are being tempted. To dream that you are selling apples indicates which you are strolling difficult for what you have. To dream of apple cider symbolizes a glowing trade. To dream of apple pie indicates wholesomeness and domestic bliss. To dream of an apple orchard suggests which you are surrounded via supportive buddies and family. Seeing a rotten apple in your dream indicates deception and betrayal. Dreaming of a crabapple indicates that you feel pissed off and discouraged.

Aquarium

Dreaming of an aquarium signifies new beginnings and excellent exchange. If you look at fish to your dream, it symbolizes happiness and abundance. Dreaming of an aquarium also can be a sign that you need to pay greater attention in your physical and emotional fitness.

Architecture

To dream of structure suggests which you are exploring your internal self and studying your spiritual beliefs and values. The dream may also be a metaphor for the manner you're building your existence.

Army

A dream of the navy indicates that you are feeling overwhelmed or threatened by way of the use of way of a few issue of your existence. The dream may be a caution to arise for yourself and take motion.

Arrow

Seeing or taking pix an arrow in your desires suggests the strength of communication. You have the capability to specific yourself definitely and straight away, with none filter out.

Asylum

To dream of an asylum method which you are unwell or have had terrible topics occur to you which you cannot get over without an entire lot of highbrow paintings.

Astral

Astrological desires show that your efforts and goals will make you well-known and a hit anywhere inside the worldwide. A ghost or a imaginative and prescient out of your astral month makes things difficult.

Atlas

To dream which you are searching at an atlas manner that you can take it sluggish in advance than making any adjustments or movements.

Atonement

It method having a exquisite time collectively with your friends and not having to worry approximately your stocks taking location.

Kids' courts for youngsters can be crowned with happiness. Women who've this dream are knowledgeable that they may be shamed through their very personal actions or the movements in their buddies due to the truth they did now not do what they were purported to.

Attic

A dream in that you are in an attic approach that you have hopes that won't come proper.

For a greater youthful girl to dream that she is snoozing in an attic manner that she might not be satisfied on the facet of her mission.

Auction

I suppose that auctions in elegant are particular. This is a superb element to do while you dream. If you pay attention the auctioneer yelling approximately his income, it approach right business organisation potentialities and straightforward remedy.

Good good fortune to the farmer with the livestock if you dream of buying them at an public sale. It's horrible for the customers. Many housewives are a terrible signal for women, however no longer all of them. In this example, you want to be careful collectively together with your business.

August

If you notice August to your desires, you may now not be able to come to an agreement or apprehend each distinctive in love.

People who assume they will get married in August are sad on the begin of their marriage.

Augur

It technique that you may want to paintings and be tired.

Aunt

Seeing your aunt in a dream way that you will get loads of scolding in case you do some thing that makes you very sad.

If this parent seems satisfied, a small exchange will fast trade into delight.

I may additionally have a drink.

To dream about talking approximately the air of mystery technique that you may have intellectual problems and are looking to decide out what strength is interior of you.

Autumn

Having a dream approximately autumn approach that she can get the property due to the efforts of various folks who want it. If she thinks approximately getting married inside the fall, she should get married and characteristic a satisfied home.

Awake

When you dream which you're giant wakeful, topics will show up at the manner to make you flow dark.

It method that you will pass inexperienced, growing fields for your dreams, and that the environment to your desires will wake up you. There is good and moderate in store for you, but there can be disappointments between now and then.

Amputation

Ordinary amputation of limbs technique that a person has out of area a small task; if someone loses every legs or each hands, it way that the alternate is in problem. After this dream, nobody must be advised to be greater cautious. Storms and out of place belongings take location all of the time for sailors.

Andirons

If you observe andirons in a dream, it way which you and your friends receives alongside. If you be conscious andirons in an empty chimney, it manner that you will lose coins and die.

Anecdote

If you dream which you're telling an anecdote, it way that you'll be happier with folks that aren't smart than with parents which is probably clever.

She may be one of the folks who revel in having amusing.

Angels

A dream approximately angels is a sign of hassle inside the soul. When it happens, it adjustments how things are going for the individual in their life. If you have got an exquisite dream, you will find out approximately humans you probably did now not realise.

If the dream is a warning, the individual that sees it could assume threats of scandal over love or money if it comes. For the wicked, it is a name to trade; for the proper people, it should be an great element.

Anger

People who've irritated goals are going to have a hard time. Loved ones who do not such as you or enemies who do no longer like you could make new attacks on you.

Seeing friends or circle of relatives being indignant with you in a dream is an indication that you will be capable of mediate among two pals and earn their lengthy-time period take transport of as actual with.

Angling

It's suitable to dream about catching fish. If you do now not get it, it's going to harm you.

Antelope

When you dream approximately seeing antler-covered antelopes, it technique that your goals might be high, but you could collect them by the usage of giving off a number of electricity.

She will apprehend that the love she wishes is long gone at the same time as she sees an antelope lose its foot and fall from a top.

Ants

During the day, the ant dreamer will ought to deal with a number of small inconveniences and be satisfied or indignant when they do now not get what they need.

Anvil

Seeing warm iron flying with sparks is an indication of pleasant artwork, an terrific harvest for the farmer, and appropriate facts for ladies. Those who are in charge can anticipate to get cold or small favors. If the anvil is broken, it way that you have possibilities that can't be not noted. The way of fulfillment are internal your attain, but you can need to paintings tough to get them.

anxiety

A dream of this kind may be unique or horrible, counting on what the dreamer cares approximately. If the dreamer cares approximately their business company, it way lousy corporation and social conditions.

Chapter 11: Appearance

Take care of what you may. In the destiny, terrible things will appear to you and your circle of relatives. Both your home and your life are in chance. Young people want to have smooth rights after they meet people of the alternative sex. To rate the character, you can give them a reduction.

Apples

For most humans, that is a amazing dream.

The sight of pink apples on trees with green feathers is sufficient to make a person dream.

Meals do no longer all taste the same, besides they're the exceptional. A pal of mine who interprets goals informed me this:

The time has come at the way to understand your goals; endure in mind what you need to do and pass with out fear.

This way, you tell him to keep his eyes down. Apples on the ground recommend that you'll be harm through fake pals and those who try to make you appearance amazing.

Bad apples are a sign of unruly art work. "

Artichoke

A dream of ingesting artichokes predicts unhappiness in amorous affairs. They also are a sign that you will go through losses if you are engaged in any hypothesis.

Aspirin

Taking aspirin on your dream suggests which you need to are searching out for treatment from a few emotional ache or anxiety that you feel.

Assassin

To dream of an assassin way that someone is making an attempt to harm or smash what you have got labored so tough for. There is a hazard lurking in your life which you want to be aware about.

Asteroid

Asteroid: To dream of an asteroid suggests a prime alternate or upheaval this is heading your way. Be prepared for the sudden.

asteroid belt.

A dream of an asteroid belt indicates that you're feeling misplaced and unsure approximately your destiny. You may be feeling beaten through the picks which you need to make.

astronaut

The dream of being an astronaut indicates that you feel constrained or restricted in some issue of your existence. You can also revel in along with you are not able to simply explicit your self or acquire your desires.

Atlantis

A dream of Atlantis suggests a time of religious growth and enlightenment. You are equipped to discover the depths of your psyche and study extra approximately your internal self.

atomic bomb

To dream of an atomic bomb shows that you feel beaten or threatened with the aid of using some trouble of your existence. The dream may be a caution to upward push up for yourself and take movement.

Attic

To dream of an attic indicates forgotten recollections and past studies which can be resurfacing. There can be some unfinished organization or issues that you want to address.

Auction

To dream of an auction suggests a time when you may need to make quick alternatives about important subjects. You can also moreover experience rushed or below pressure to offer you a solution.

Apricot

To see apricots growing for your dream approach that the destiny, although it looks like it is going to be a extraordinary time, has bitterness and hidden sorrow for you.

Consumption is an indication that horrific things are about to occur. If different humans maintain doing this, the surroundings becomes unsightly and no longer conducive in your fantasies.

Apricots imply that you spent an excessive amount of time on matters that were not crucial.

April

It way you will have quite some fun. If the climate is unhappy, it manner that horrible subjects are coming.

Apron

If you're a younger woman, you want to take a complex route to get your apron again. If you are a trainer, fantasizing about taking down or smashing your desk effects in horrible commands approximately the health of mother and father and teachers.

Ransom

If you dream that a ransom has been paid for you, you'll discover that you're being ripped off and taking walks for money on all sides.

For a younger woman, it's far a terrible sign besides a person can pay the ransom and frees her.

Grated

Having this dream technique that some of your buddies are going to be very unhappy.

That will harm her pride and make her boyfriend split collectively along side her.

Fast

Thinking which you are being carried away thru rapids in a dream manner that you're going to lose a whole lot of cash because you did no longer do your assignment and searched for topics that had been a laugh.